SCOTTISH RAILWAY
Connections

Stanier 'Coronation' Class No. 46242 "City of Glasgow"

Built at the Crewe Works of the London Midland & Scottish Railway at a cost of £10,838 it entered service on 15 May 1940.
Classified 7P the locomotive was originally built as a streamlined Pacific but the casing was removed in March 1947.
Reclassified 8P under British Railways it was withdrawn from service in October 1963.

NARRATIVE BY BOB CRAMPSEY

PUBLISHED BY

THE GLASGOW ROYAL CONCERT HALL

FOREWORD BY LORD WHITELAW

ARTWORK BY DUGALD CAMERON

First published in Great Britain in 1994 by
The Glasgow Royal Concert Hall
2 Sauchiehall Street
Glasgow G2 3NY

ISBN 0 9522174 1 4

A catalogue record for this book is available from the British Library

Design and production by Alan Carlaw

Typeset by Squadron Prints Ltd, Giffnock, Glasgow
Printed by Elpeeko Ltd, Lincoln

Foreword
by
Lord Whitelaw

"Scottish Railway Connections"

"Famous Ships of the Clyde", published by The Glasgow Royal Concert Hall, has proved a most valuable and enjoyable contribution to Scottish history, and to the Clyde in particular.

It is followed by "Scottish Railway Connections", which is of special interest to me, as my Grandfather, William Whitelaw, was in turn, Chairman of the Highland Railway, The North British Railway and after the major railway amalgamation in Britain, of the LNER – some 40 years in all. And so as a boy, I heard many stories from him about the remarkable achievements of all those Scotsmen who built the railways and produced the engines which ran on them. Their skill and determination provided essential communications in very difficult country, such as the West Highland line.

"Scottish Railway Connections" portrays a fascinating study of the Scottish development, which will tell us much about the spirit and inventiveness of our Scottish forebears.

LNER A1 class pacific No. 2563 "William Whitelaw" was built by the N B Loco Co and entered service in July 1924.
It was initially allocated to Cowlairs shed but moved to Doncaster in 1931. It was renamed "Tagalie" in August 1941

AUTHOR'S PREFACE

Let me break with custom by discouraging customers. Let me tell you what this book is not. Should buffer-beams loom largely in your life then read no further. If a compelling interest is the Jumper Blast Pipe then, "Horseman, pass by." This book is non-technical, I lack the effrontery to have essayed such a book.

If, however, you marvel like me that Scots and Scotland should have been so much involved with arguably the most far-reaching invention of the nineteenth century, indeed, could fairly claim European pre-eminence for the last quarter of that century and well beyond, then you will find Scottish Railway Connections of interest.

What this book *is* may be described as an attempt to pay tribute to those marvellous Victorians and Edwardians who, in producing what was essentially functional, so often achieved that which was beautiful.

Age has its compensations and to be the other side of 60 is to remember the railway steamers in their pre-1939 pomp, to have seen the *Coronation Scot* long before Vivian Ellis's music immortalised it, to have travelled the Waverley line and to have gone to Prestwick on the famous "golfer's train" in those last days before Hitler.

Others will have different recollections but I hope that pictures, paintings and text will convince younger readers that it could be said of Springburn as of Camelot – (an unlikely conjunction) – that "once there was a fleeting wisp of glory."

Bob Brampsey

The author and publisher would like to thank Dr Ann Glen and Morrison Bryce for their technical research and final detailed check before publication of this book.

Night Mail

(Commentary for a GPO film)
by Wystan Hugh Auden
reproduced by courtesy of Faber and Faber

This is the Night Mail crossing the Border,
Bringing the cheque and the postal order,

Letters for the rich, letters for the poor,
The shop at the corner, the girl next door.

Pulling up Beattock, a steady climb:
The gradient's against her, but she's on time.

Past cotton-grass and moorland border,
Shovelling white steam over her shoulder.

Snorting noisily, she passes
Silent miles of wind-bent grasses.

Birds turn their heads as she approaches,
Stare from the bushes at her blank-faced coaches.

Sheep-dogs cannot turn her course;
They slumber on with paws across.

In the farm she passes no one wakes,
But a jug in a bedroom gently shakes.

II
Dawn freshens. Her climb is done.
Down towards Glasgow she descends,
Towards the steam tugs yelping down a glade of cranes,
Towards the fields of apparatus, the furnaces
Set on the dark plain like gigantic chessmen.
All Scotland waits for her:
In dark glens, beside pale-green lochs,
Men long for news.

III
Letters of thanks, letters from banks,
Letters of joy from girl and boy,
Receipted bills and invitations
To inspect new stock or to visit relations,
And applications for situations,
And timid lovers' declarations,
And gossip, gossip from all the nations,
News circumstantial, new financial,
Letters with holiday snaps to enlarge in,
Letters with faces scrawled in the margin,
Letters from uncles, cousins and aunts,
Letters to Scotland from the South of France,
Letters of condolence to Highlands and Lowlands,
Written on paper of every hue,
The pink, the violet, the white and the blue,
The chatty, the catty, the boring, the adoring,
The cold and official and the heart's outpouring,
Clever, stupid, short and long,
The typed and the printed and the spelt all wrong.

IV
Thousands are still asleep,
Dreaming of terrifying monsters
Or a friendly tea beside the band in Cranston's or Crawford's:
Asleep in working Glasgow, asleep in well-set Edinburgh,
Asleep in granite Aberdeen,
They continue their dreams,
But shall wake soon and hope for letters,
And none will hear the postman's knock
Without a quickening of the heart.
For who can bear to feel himself forgotten?

The West Coast Postal
© Dugald Cameron

BARCLAY'S OF KILMARNOCK

Few things could have seemed less likely than that a small Kilmarnock engineering firm, of which the financial affairs were in a constant state of turmoil, would live to see off the great North British Locomotive Company so that it would eventually end up as the last locomotive manufacturer in Scotland.

The initial chaos was largely due to the personality of the founder, Andrew Barclay, a fine engineer with a truly inventive mind but a rather less secure grasp of business principles.

He was born in Dalry, Ayrshire in 1814 and after a few months in a carpet factory in Kilmarnock he served his apprenticeship in that town in a plumber and tinsmith's. By 1840 he had gone into partnership with Thomas McCulloch manufacturing mill shafting.

Bankruptcy and sequestration proceedings met him for the first but far from the last time in 1847 when he was able to carry on by selling his new gasolier invention to his principal creditor.

By the middle 1850s he had taken over the Titchfield Foundry and the step from colliery and factory machinery to locomotives was a natural one, although at 44 years of age he had left his entry to this arena rather late. Through a network of companies, Barclay and Co, A Barclay Sons and Co Ltd, he built locomotives at two factories in the town, the Riverbank and the Caledonia.

Whenever Andrew Barclay was doing well he could be depended upon to over-reach himself and his involvement in the Cumberland-based Lonsdale Haematite Iron Company proved too great a financial burden. As before a leading creditor esteemed him greatly as an engineer if not as a businessman. This time a Glasgow ironmaster, Thomas Steven bailed him out.

In his time Andrew Barclay would be sequestrated, or the attempt to have him so made, on five occasions. His creditors were also worried about his passion for astronomy, maintaining that he devoted far too much time and money to the building of a giant telescope. His was no mere amateur dabbling however, when interested members of the Royal Astronomical Society came to see the instrument, Barclay was nominated for a fellowship almost immediately.

Industrial tank engines were the firm's stock in trade and they remained so when Barclay died in 1900, combative and litigious to the end. Kilmarnock was however nothing if not versatile. From its yards came the locomotives for the Campbeltown and Machrihanish Light Railway, engines for private colliery lines such as the Wemyss Private Railway in Fife, fireless engines for use in munitions works, refineries and other areas of high explosive risk. In these last instances the boiler of the locomotive was charged with steam from static boilers. Barclay engines could also be found on the narrow-gauge British Aluminium Company's line which ran for 21 miles between Loch Treig and Loch Linnhe in Inverness-shire.

In all the company built well over 2000 0-4-0 and 0-6-0 tank engines whose only defect was that they were almost too durable, many recording half a century of service. There were bulk orders of 25 0-6-0s for the War Office (the connection with the Ministry of Defence is an ongoing one) and the same quantity was provided for the LMS between the wars.

There was heavy penetration of the English market and Ayrshire locomotives could be found in Peru, the West Indies, China, Egypt and the logging camps of Australia. It was fitting that the very last steam order fulfilled by Barclay's in 1962 was an 0-6-2 for Indonesia.

That was the year in which the NB Loco works finally closed its Glasgow doors and greatly daring, Barclay's bid to take over the goodwill of the defunct company. This bold stroke was almost as if Ealing Studios had tendered for the goodwill of MGM in the 1950s and the far-sightedness met with deserved success and immediately revitalised order books.

Barclay's retained the facility for steam locomotive work until 1974. Two years before that they had become part of the Hunslet Group, a move which brought them some advanced diesel work. The Kilmarnock works were well prepared for this as they had begun to experiment with diesel engines as far back as 1935.

The link with the narrow gauge railways was maintained in 1991 with the delivery of an 0-4-0 engine for the Snowdon rack and pinion railway while at the same time the company was building 3-Car electric multiple units for British Rail. As Andrew Barclay looks down through his celestial telescope he is no doubt smiling wryly as he reflects that it was a comparatively unlikely horse that successfully stayed the distance.

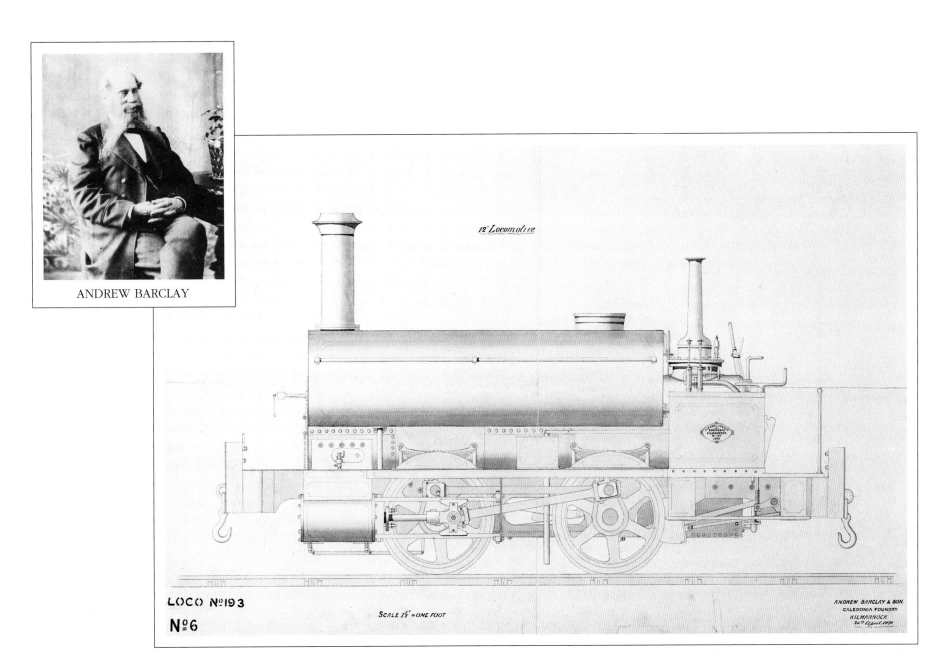

ANDREW BARCLAY

12" Locomotive

LOCO Nº193

Nº6

SCALE 1½" = ONE FOOT

ANDREW BARCLAY & SON.
CALEDONIA FOUNDRY
KILMARNOCK

LOCOMOTIVE No. 193

Built in 1878 for the Clippens Oil Co Ltd, Midlothian it operated on colliery lines and passed to the NCB in 1947 before being scrapped in 1954.
The drawing is one of the earliest to survive in the Company archives.

© Hunslet-Barclay

DUGALD DRUMMOND

Dugald Drummond, perhaps even more than Walter Neilson, has a firm claim to be known as the stormy petrel of Scottish locomotive engineering. Born at Ardrossan in 1840, he served his apprenticeship with the Glasgow firm of Forrest and Barr. Almost his first railway experience was on the Dunbartonshire Railway where his father was a Permanent Way Inspector. While still a young man he worked in England with Peto, Brassey and Betts, highly reputable locomotive builders in Birkenhead. He had the good fortune early on to work with such a luminary as William Stroudley at Cowlairs, at Inverness with the Highland Railway, and Brighton, serving in effect three terms of duty with the great man.

In 1875 he became Locomotive Superintendent for the North British Railway at Cowlairs and at once proceeded to tackle what he saw as the outstanding problems. Chief of these was a rag-bag of classes of engines in use that needed standardisation. He was strongly influenced by Stroudley although the general opinion is that his robust locomotives were a breakthrough.

His most innovative work was the introduction of a dozen 4-4-0 passenger engines for the London St Pancras – Edinburgh line using the Waverley route through Hawick which persisted into the 1960s. In the last twenty years of the nineteenth century the Drummond 4-4-0s brooked no rivals on this line. They maintained a cracking pace, although the most desperate piece of speeding was achieved by a special train in 1916 pulling only one coach which covered the distance from Edinburgh to Carlisle in just 105 minutes for the 98.5 miles. A senior military officer had missed his train and chartered a special in desperation to rejoin his own train (and eventually his unit) at Carlisle. How had he come to miss it? A high-level conference? An affair of the heart? We will never know.

Drummond had the temperament that would "start a row in an empty house" as the Scots phrase has it and in 1882 he moved across the fence to the Caledonian Railway works at St Rollox and the famous Caledonian No. 123 was built during his spell there by Neilson's.

His restlessness continued with a short and pretty unsuccessful foray to Australia. At fifty years old he would today have been looking for retirement or had the choice made for him but things were different in the 1890s. His locomotive firm, founded in Glasgow on his return from Australia, attracted few commissions and those mostly for industrial engines, although the Company did better when his sons took over. Originally located in Helen Street in Govan, it moved to the Carntyne district and was making wheels and axles until shortly before its close in 1958.

Long long before that in 1895 at the age of 55 Drummond had become Chief Mechanical Engineer to the London & South Western Railway.

The years had not dimmed his powers of invention. He experimented with crossed water tubes in the fire boxes and he produced a revolutionary spark arrester. And all the while he fought his staff and sacked them, and feathers flew.

He was a born commander. He supervised the removal of the L & S W's main workshops from the hopelessly congested Nine Elms in London to the comparative spaciousness of Eastleigh in Hampshire. The Drummond 4-4-0s hauled the hugely prestigious American boat trains to Southampton for years. Some of his T9 engines were running more than 50 years after their construction.

A fascinating man, if one's weekly pay packet was not dependent on him. Although capable of surprising spasms of leniency, first-offence drunkenness warranted only a "yellow card" in modern terms, there is little doubt that he was a real Victorian "driver" whose word was law.

His death was in keeping with his life. He scalded himself, paid no attention to the scald, gangrene set in and he died in November 1912. Railway legend has it that his men placed half a ton of brake blocks on top of his coffin to prevent a return journey but his real memorial will be the graceful *Abbotsford* class which for so long adorned the principal North British lines and his engines for the Caley and the L & S W Railway.

DUGALD DRUMMOND

DRUMMOND'S JUMBOS

The Caledonian Railway Co's order No. E561 to Neilson & Co on 27 December 1882 called for 15 Goods Engines & Tenders to Dugald Drummond's design.
No.294, the first, was delivered on 13 November 1883 and continued in service until withdrawn in July 1962 as BR No.57249.

WALTER NEILSON

Walter Montgomerie Neilson was one of the great Scottish triumvirate of locomotive builders in the late nineteenth century, the others being James Reid and Henry Dübs, the last named was a German who had settled in Scotland.

Neilson had succeeded to a family business in the Anderston district of Glasgow which concentrated on making factory engines – pumping engines, condensing engines, sugar mills and the like.

Walter Neilson saw immediately that the future lay with locomotives and by 1852 he had exported his first engine, to Cuba. Tremendously inventive he even designed an ice locomotive for Russia, steered by a wheel and intended to run on frozen snow. In the 1850s Neilson took Dübs into partnership and allowed his then foreman, James Reid, to go to Sharp, Stewart of Manchester to fill the same post.

The partnership with Dübs initially flourished. Neilson was determined that he would break the English monopoly in locomotive manufacture and although conceding that centres like Manchester had got the start he saw no reason why they could not be overhauled. He refused all suggestions that his own career might lie in the South. "If the engines cannot be made by me in Glasgow and by Scotchmen too, they will never be made by me in England."

Within a short time he had so overcome the twin difficulties of geographical remoteness and English hostility to purchasing from him that his engines were going to South America, Africa and a dozen European counties. The original premises at Stobcross had long ceased to be adequate and he now operated from the Hyde Park works in Springburn.

He seems, even from his own unpublished memoir, to have been a difficult, curiously unworldly man and he now fell out with Dübs who set up for himself in the Polmadie district in the mid 1860s.

Neilson plugged the gap by bringing back James Reid from Manchester who was not only a gifted engineer but an infinitely better business man. He negotiated a partnership which gave him the right to buy out Neilson after 10 years and he duly claimed performance of it. Neilson, bitter and mortified, wrote that "he (Reid) took every shilling out of my pocket that it was possible for him to do." It is impossible for us to judge the fairness of this condemnation as no written rebuttal appears to exist. One may say in passing that James Reid did appear to possess the necessary quality of luck, even his death was the perfect one for a Scotsman as it occurred while he was attempting to recover from a bunker on the Old Course at St Andrews!

Neilson left Scotland for a while but returned in 1884 to open "a shop across the street" from Hyde Park. His initial success was once again not sustained and in 1888 he was glad enough to sell out to Sharp, Stewart of Manchester who re-named the new works the Atlas Works after their own premises in Manchester. Among the orders taken over was one for eight locomotives for the Brazilian Government.

Walter Montgomerie Neilson was perhaps a better engineer than a businessman and he was clearly difficult to work with, his life is littered with feuds and misjudgements of men. He had great gifts of invention and deserves our remembrance for his efforts to maintain Scotland in the forefront of locomotive engineering manufacture and design. He was not the first Scot, - nor the last-, as John Logie Baird and George Bennie of Rail-plane fame would have testified, to have received scant reward for his pre-eminent inventive skills.

WALTER NEILSON

INDUSTRIAL TANK ENGINE

A single-cylinder industrial tank locomotive designed by Neilson pictured outside the works in Anderston before moving to Springburn

BEARDMORE'S OF DALMUIR

Most Scots would connect Beardmore's of Dalmuir with ships of war and heavy ordnance rather than with locomotives and it is true that the great enterprise started life in 1906 as a Naval Yard, caught up in the flurry of European competition to build *Dreadnought* battleships in those last hectic pre-1914 years.

At the peak of the First World War, the firm of William Beardmore employed more than 40,000 people in its various enterprises and was largely responsible for the development of the town of Clydebank but with the armistice of 1918 the armaments trade collapsed. Worse, unrivalled British naval supremacy had gone for ever, no longer was parity with the next two strongest naval powers combined a priority of foreign policy.

How to keep the splendid plant at Dalmuir productive and the skilled work-force employed? The answer was to turn to locomotive building. This involved the alteration of buildings at Dalmuir with cranes increased in size and capacity and walls strengthened to bear heavier loads.

By 1920 Dalmuir was producing locomotives. It had certain advantages, chief of which was its location on the Clyde so that locomotives could be loaded on board ship ready for service. The company became very adept at this, on a single day in 1925 no fewer than 25 locomotives were swung aboard in just 14.5 hours.

This saved the tortuous trail through city streets which the rival works of Hyde Park and Queen's Park faced and greatly reduced the necessity for dismantling and crating.

The story of Beardmore's as a locomotive works is one of a narrow failure. In the 10 years between 1920– 30 almost 400 locomotives were built and of these 393 nearly half (192) went abroad. India was by far the biggest overseas market but there were also orders for Nigeria and Burma, indeed the five Mallet locomotives built for Burma Railways were possibly the most interesting and individual productions for the big 0-6-6-0 locomotives were extremely successful.

It was one thing to manufacture engines for the Colonies and Dominions, where Crown Agents did the ordering, quite another thing to break into the fiercer foreign markets. Had a huge order for 200 locomotives for Roumania been landed in the mid-1920s (and it very nearly was) then the yard's chances of survival would have been that much better. As it was, not even two respectable orders from the London and North Western Railway in 1921 and the London Midland and Scottish in 1927 could keep things afloat.

It was not that craftsmanship was deficient in any aspect. Beardmore's was asked to build a *Prince of Wales* class 4-6-0 for the LMS to display at the Empire Exhibition of 1924 at Wembley. The engine, numbered 5845 and bearing the name of the class it represented, was the subject of much approving comment.

Perhaps the Company had entered the locomotive business too late, perhaps it lacked the necessary contacts. Perhaps it was the usual Scottish handicap of comparatively remote industrial location, perhaps it was because Dalmuir was such an expensively-equipped yard and plant that profitability was always going to be difficult.

Whatever the reason, by 1930 the Naval Yard was closed and locomotive manufacturing ceased. The great ships had been built for only 25 years and the powerful locomotives for ten. Beardmore's had seemed a planet in the Scottish industrial sky and yet Dalmuir had scarcely operated for the years needed for son to succeed father as a time-served journeyman. The great post-war slump, prolonged and universal, had done for the enterprise and it was a heart-broken William Beardmore who died in April 1936, when even his elevation to the peerage as Lord Invernairn was of little consolation to him.

WILLIAM BEARDMORE

GREAT EASTERN RAILWAY 4-6-0

Designed by S D Holden, this 'S69' class No. 1560 was built at Dalmuir in April 1921

© Ian Johnston

SPRINGBURN – RAILWAY ENGINES FOR THE WORLD

It is a reflection of the justice of its claim to be the Second City of the Empire that Glasgow in the 40 years or so prior to 1914 had two of the three largest locomotive manufacturing works in Europe, let alone Britain, and in addition there was a third considerable establishment on the south side of the river Clyde.

The Springburn situation was truly phenomenal. There were four major works and two huge loco depots. Of the works, two were privately owned and two were operated by the Scottish railway companies (North British & Caledonian) themselves.

Of the latter the Saint Rollox works was the property of the Caledonian Railway which always used the full title of sanctity, the abbreviation came with the grouping of 1923. Here were built the magnificent Caley blue engines. Along the road at Cowlairs lay the works of the North British Railway, the first establishment to be owned by a Scottish railway company. The engines fabricated here were bronze green, a rivalry that was to be oddly duplicated in that other obsession of the work force, Association Football.

As for the private owners the Hyde Park works of Neilson Reid & Co employed 3,275 hands at a time when no English workshop could claim more than two thousand. Another concern the Atlas Works which Sharp, Stewart of Manchester had purchased from Walter Neilson (changing the name from Clyde Works) employed almost 1,600 people at the turn of the century. When these two works combined with that of Henry Dübs in 1903 to form the North British Locomotive Company its scale was only surpassed in the United States. The Polmadie establishment of Dübs was properly called N.B. Locomotive Co (Queen's Park) but in my boyhood in the 1930s it was invariably referred to as "Dubbs", juvenile Southsiders being convinced that the owner had been a double 'B'.

Springburn ate, slept and dreamt railways. Anyone who doubts that should consider the incredible "works outing" of September 1899 when 15,000 people (more than half the population) occupying 252 coaches and pulled by 14 Springburn-built Dunalastairs were transported to Carlisle and back for payment of the modest shilling.

The first 4-6-0 to run in Britain was built at Springburn, so too, as has been said were the powerful Dunalastairs. It was, however, the exported locomotives which aroused the greatest communal interest. Going all over the world as they did, the one thing they often had in common was a non-conformity to British Standard Gauge and thus an inability to move to the docks on rails. They were therefore almost always taken through the city streets on low loaders at dead of night, but they seldom if ever departed unwitnessed, large and enthusiastic crowds saw them on their way.

It was always likely that the post World War One trend to rationalisation would adversely affect Springburn and so it proved. Grouping took place in 1923 by which time Cowlairs was no longer building locomotives. The bad years of the 1930s further exacerbated matters and the Atlas Works was especially severely hit. But for the re-armament of the late 1930s it would certainly have closed but survived on the twin diet of war-time railway expansion and armament making.

The end of Springburn as a major force in the manufacture of locomotives came with appalling suddenness. There had been an upsurge after the return of peace in 1945 and double-shift working was the order of the day as countries strove to replenish their war-battered and neglected engines. But the days of steam were numbered and the Springburn new romance with the diesel was ill-starred. There were severe difficulties with the first batch of diesel engines entrusted to the workshops there and Springburn never recovered from the adverse publicity incurred.

It may have been that the managers and men were slow to see that steam had gone for ever. It may have been that since they were lovers of steam and craftsmen to their fingertips that they simply could not muster any great enthusiasm for the new methods.

No matter the reason by 1962 the North British Locomotive Company was in receivership. Cowlairs closed its doors in 1968 and the site is now occupied by an industrial estate, an ironical term in a Glasgow that is now nothing if not post-industrial. St Rollox alone survived, diminished in stature as in name, to become the Springburn depot of British Rail Maintenance Ltd. Today a hard-to-find gatepost, a carved stone over a door, provide the fugitive proofs that this was once a place where thousands worked at an occupation in which they called no man, anywhere, their superior.

COWLAIRS WORKS

Main erecting shop with 'S' class locomotives under construction in 1921

THE SCOTTISH CONTRIBUTION TO THE MAKING OF THE CPR

Normally the benefits conferred by the building of a railway line are social and economic. In the case of the Canadian Pacific Railway, in the building of which the Scottish influence was vital and profound, the completion of the line brought the gift of nationhood itself.

Canada in 1867 was a hotchpotch of provinces racked by hostility between Upper (Ontario) and Lower (Quebec) and the legacy of Anglo-French bitterness while the young United States of America, freed of its Civil War, was casting covetous eyes to the north and west. The newly constituted province of British Columbia had declared in 1871 that it would only adhere to the Confederation if there was a trans-continental railway in existence within ten years.

The CPR was built by the toil and heroism of Irish navvies and contractors but it was a group of Scots who supplied the financial backing and the political determination to see the scheme through to a successful conclusion. Chief of these was Sir John A Macdonald, lawyer, politician and Prime Minister whose enthusiasm for the railway caused him to be involved in a scandal which temporarily drove him from office. Sir Hugh Allan was the invaluable contacts man, Donald A Smith and George Stephen the influential members of the "Scotch Montreal Group" which pushed the venture onwards and Sir Sandford Fleming was the chief engineer in the great enterprise. Each of these men will be noticed individually later.

The government had made a half-hearted effort to begin operations immediately after Confederation in 1867 but it soon became apparent that the matter was better left to private enterprise. The Scots in Canada were pre-eminently influential in the fur trade (the Hudson's Bay Company was at one time almost a Scottish preserve), banking and government. The Lowland Scots work ethic and their willingness to defer spending and gratification made them ideal for the purpose of great engineering enterprises.

To build the railway meant overcoming the hostility of the native peoples, the climate and the geological problems set by the formidable Canadian Shield and by the ranges of the Rockies.

The original route was to take the line into the Western terminal, Vancouver, by the Thomson and Fraser rivers and the Yellowhead Pass, but in the end a more southerly route was chosen than Sandford Fleming had suggested. This was real pioneering work for when Fleming and his men surveyed Kicking Horse Pass they were probably the first white men to have traversed the district since Captain Palliser and Jamie Hector whose misadventure with a horse caused the pass to be so named.

The last spike was driven by Donald A Smith himself at Eagle Pass at a spot thereupon called Craigellachie to mark the fact that Smith's roots, like those of Stephen, were in the north-east of Scotland. It was no coincidence that the chief holiday resort of the Canadian Rockies would bear the name of Banff Springs. The work had been completed five years ahead of the deadline set by the federal government.

By the end of the century, the CPR had begun to build its notable fleet of liners which would connect Scotland with Canada and as early as 1937 the first diesel-electric locomotive ran on its tracks. By the Second World War the company had become involved with air transport, and today it operates railroad tracks in the United States which go as far south as Kansas City and Louisville, Kentucky. The shady election deals of 1872, the political manoeuvring, the inter-provincial and inter-party jealousies ended in the birth of one of the great railways of the world and the Scots self-denying proverb "Work, save, study — study, save, work" had brought the great project to fruition.

SIR DONALD SMITH
Reminiscing with Father Lacombe, one of the first missionaries in the North-West.
It was he who persuaded Chief Crowfoot not to oppose the railroad.

SIR HUGH ALLAN

SIR JOHN MACDONALD

SIR SANDFORD FLEMING

SIR GEORGE STEPHEN

THE FIVE SCOTS WHO BUILT THE RAILROAD

SIR JOHN ALEXANDER MACDONALD (1815 – 1891)

Sir John A Macdonald was born in Glasgow in 1815 but lived almost all his life in Canada, being taken there at the age of five. He chose the law as his profession and was called to the bar when he was twenty-one years old. His overwhelming desire was to make a nation out of the separate and fractious provinces that made up British North America in the early nineteenth century.

To this end he was quick to see the advantages of a trans-continental railway system. Indeed, his zeal for this objective led to his temporary departure from public life in 1873 when he was accused of taking large donations to his Conservative Party in 1872 from another Scot, Sir Hugh Allan (qv).

The sums had been given in return for access to the St Paul line which was needed to monopolise North-Western traffic and in addition Allan was angling for the charter to construct the CPR.

Macdonald, a noted conciliator, who was the prime mover in the Confederation or Union of 1867 which declared Canada a nation, survived the scandal and was returned to office. Not even heavy drinking, private and not infrequently semi-public, could alienate the affections of the voters and when he suffered a stroke in 1891, the newspaper headlines "He is dying" required no further explanation. The man had become the nation.

SIR GEORGE STEPHEN, LORD MOUNT STEPHEN (1829 — 1921)

George Stephen together with his cousin Donald A Smith was mainly instrumental in carrying the building of the great Canadian railway to a successful conclusion. He was born at Dufftown in Banffshire and after some time in London arrived in Canada in 1850. His early career was in the drapery trade and in woollens but such was his ability to learn and capacity for hard work that by 1873 he had become vice-president of the Bank of Montreal, the largest Canadian bank, and three years later he was its president.

His interest in railways dated from this time for he bought out the Dutch holders of the St Paul and Pacific Railway and it was very largely the same syndicate which undertook in 1880 the task of building a line to the west coast.

Stephen himself ascribed his success to effort rather than genius. "I had neither the training nor talent to accomplish anything without hard work and fortunately I knew it." Observers spoke of his "personal pluck, intrepidity and magnetism".

He lived to be President of the CPR and his title, Lord Mount Stephen (he had been knighted in 1886) was taken from a peak in the Rocky Mountains named after him while he was President of that Company. He spent most of his later life back in Britain.

Donald Smith driving the last spike into the CPR at Craigellachie, 7 November 1885
© Mitchell Library

SIR DONALD A SMITH, LORD STRATHCONA AND MOUNT ROYAL (1820 – 1914)

Donald A Smith, a cousin of George Stephen was born in the Spey Valley in 1820 and joined the Hudson's Bay Company when he was 18 years old. His early Canadian years were spent in Labrador and the North-West and he rose to be first of all Chief Factor and eventually Chief Commissioner of the Company. He spent many years as an MP but when Macdonald fell from power over the Pacific Scandal of 1873 Smith became a Liberal. He never lost touch with the former Prime Minister however and on his return to power supported him on a personal basis.

Smith was an alley fighter who well knew how to raise money and how to apply pressure. He had no self-doubt and was a terrifyingly formidable negotiator.

His place in railway history would have been secure had he done no more than drive the last spike of the CPR. His latter days contained one humorous element. In 1897, about to be elevated to the peerage, it was discovered that he not been properly married although he had a wife of some fifty years standing. He had married her however according to Labrador custom, i.e. without the presence of a clergyman as such were hard to find in that vast unpeopled territory. The man whose frowns made governments tremble meekly complied with the Establishment's insistence and was officially married in the British Embassy in Paris at 77 years of age.

SIR HUGH ALLAN (1810 – 1882)

Hugh Allan was born at Saltcoats and spent his early days working in the family counting-house in Greenock. The traditional family interest had been in shipping and on going to Canada at the age of sixteen Allan first worked with a grain merchant but then set himself to acquire both ocean-going ships and coastal ships which could work the profitable Quebec–Montreal route.

There was soon a lucrative trade with Glasgow, importing manufactured goods and exporting Canadian grain. A key player in the Scotch Montreal Syndicate, he knew where finance was available to fund the construction of the CPR. By mid-century the Allan Line was perhaps the most important on the Canadian run, and in future years it would, together with the Beaver Line, be acquired by the CPR itself. He was quick to see the importance of the Pembina branch line, the connecting spur which the Canadian Government was building to the border from St Paul.

Described as "an active pushing man" he died in Edinburgh in December 1882 but it is perhaps an indication of his love for his new country that he chose to be buried in Montreal later that month.

SIR SANDFORD FLEMING (1827 – 1915)

Fleming was a Fifer born in Kirkcaldy, who studied surveying in Scotland. He was eighteen when he arrived in Canada where at an early stage he worked with Casimir Gzowski and this Polish civil engineer gave him railway experience on the Ontario, Simcoe and Huron Railroad. Fleming became Chief Railway Engineer to the provincial government of Nova Scotia and he completed the Intercolonial Railway from Montreal to Halifax in 1876.

Five years earlier he had been appointed Chief Railway Engineer for the trans-continental railway and in 1872 he had drawn up his route as indicated elsewhere. He was in charge while more than 600 miles of the route were completed but then left active operations to become a director.

As an engineer he was almost as versatile as Brunel. He was largely instrumental in the laying of the Pacific cable which linked Canada and Australia, his was the conception of Standard Time Zones for the North American continent and in addition to founding the Royal Canadian Institute, Canada's senior scientific organisation, he designed the country's first postage stamp.

THE ROYAL SCOT TRAIN

On the face of it a wonderful publicity opportunity appears to have been wasted in that the 10 o'clock Euston–Glasgow Central train was unnamed for much the better part of a century, only acquiring the title *Royal Scot* in 1927.

This was at the time when the agreement of the two companies, LMS and LNER to collaborate on journey times to the North was beginning to fray at the edges. As yet it was not possible to alter timetables so the selling point was on the length of non-stop travel during the journey.

For the first few months of 1927 and 1928 the rival lines indulged in a kind of permanent way leapfrog. The LMS drew first blood in late 1927 by running 236 miles non-stop to Carnforth in Lancashire. The LNER then riposted with a 268 mile headlong dash to Newcastle-upon-Tyne. Nothing daunted, the West Coast operators announced that they would reach Carlisle from London in one fell swoop and indeed would not even have a passenger stop there, only the crews would change over at Kingmoor signal box.

It could be argued that these antics entertained professional railwaymen more than the travelling public in the same way that scoops appeal more to newspapermen than an apathetic readership but there was more to come.

The LMS got wind that the LNER were about to introduce a non-stop service between King's Cross and Edinburgh Waverley commencing on 1 May 1928. The LMS could not follow suit on a regular timetable basis because they had to divide the Edinburgh and Glasgow sections of their train at Symington in Lanarkshire. However, on 27 April 1928, a couple of days before the epoch-making East Coast run they announced, with whatever justification, that because of exceptionally heavy traffic they were operating two separate trains for Edinburgh and Glasgow that day and would run them straight through to their respective destinations non-stop.

It was a one-off of course, but to pursue the newspaper analogy it was a great "spoiler" and caused a deal of chagrin to the LNER. The LMS non-stop record run of 401 miles to Glasgow remained the longest such journey under steam for 20 years more.

The train itself was extremely well-equipped and in particular the new first-class carriages, introduced in 1928, were much admired. Some of these had only 28 seats to allow all the occupants a window view and to enable them to dine in their seats if they so wished.

Travel times improved. By 1939 the journey could be made in seven hours and Carlisle, 299 miles from London, was reached at an average speed of a mile a minute. This commendable rate was the more easily achieved as the Stanier Pacifics began to take over the route.

One wartime oddity may be noted in that formerly a typical *Royal Scot* train coming north would have 9 Glasgow coaches, 4 Edinburgh ones and 2 for Aberdeen. During the war, as on the East Coast line the time for the trip moved back to nine hours at best. It became the wartime practice to run the Perth service and beyond separately. It was therefore possible to achieve a through journey on British mainland soil of 721 miles from Euston to Thurso. The weary *matelots* flocking back off leave to Scapa Flow, to which the great bulk of the Thurso traffic was destined, were not always sufficiently grateful for being allowed to be thus part of railway history!

THE ROYAL SCOT

Stanier Coronation class No. 46243 "City of Lancaster" heads the up Royal Scot at Bay Horse in September 1960

© A E R Cope/Colour-Rail

THE FLYING SCOTSMAN TRAIN

It is not infrequently a source of confusion when a locomotive and a train service bear the same name and in the case of the *Flying Scotsman* care needs to be taken in distinguishing one from the other. Here the train came well before the locomotive of that name. The first King's Cross – Edinburgh service was in 1862 and it set the traditional departure time of 10 am. The arrival at Edinburgh was 10½ hours later but this included a lunch stop at York and a "comfort stop" at Newcastle in those early days before dining cars and corridor trains.

The original name for the train was simply the Special Scotch Express but the better-known term was certainly in vogue well before 1890. By 1887 the running time had been brought down to 9 hours but it was the decision to allow third class passengers to use the service which really started off the Great Race of 1888. By that year the time had been reduced to 7 hours, 26 minutes and 45 seconds and this included a 26½ minute lunch stop at York which might have stayed the passengers' hunger but can have done little for their digestions.

This unbridled rivalry on the East and West coast lines was potentially dangerous and in the late 1880s an informal, unwritten agreement was reached whereby there would be no journey to Edinburgh of less than 8¼ hours. Paradoxically this decision was arrived at just as locomotives were becoming larger and more efficient with the result that the powerful engines were, comparatively speaking, dawdling on the last stretch between Berwick-on-Tweed and Edinburgh.

With the incorporation of the LNER in 1923 the King's Cross line was under unified control for the first time in its more than 60 year history. At once the company and its rival, the LMS, began to measure weapons. On 1 May 1928 the new *Flying Scotsman*, now equipped with such fripperies as a cocktail bar and a barber's salon, did the 393 mile journey non-stop.

Around this time too there was the celebrated "race" between the *Flying Scotsman* and a British Imperial Airways aircraft. It was not an actual race at all since the aircraft was supposed to pick up the train at the Royal Border Bridge at Berwick, but somehow managed to liaise with the wrong train! The fragile gentleman's agreement disintegrated and by 1939 the journey time from King's Cross to Waverley was down to 7 hours. Such a tight schedule demanded rigorous timekeeping, nowhere more so than at Grantham where the train was booked in on the half-minute and departed two minutes later on the half-minute.

The Second World War put an end to such frivolity. War restrictions, especially the black-out, put another 90 minutes back on the journey and it says much for the railwaymen that they coped with bomb damage and an inadequately maintained permanent way. If the wartime trains were slower they were often considerably larger, trains of 800 tons were by no means unknown.

The hoped-for transition to peacetime for the *Scotsman* was slow to come. All over Britain the railway system was battered, tired and worn out. The floods of August 1948 gave the East Coast line a major problem for almost two years which restricted speeds. The great train gave the townspeople of Kelso and the villagers of Coldstream an unwonted close look as it trundled slowly on its way to St Boswells, there to join the Waverley line.

In 1958 occurred the first haulage by a diesel locomotive on the route and steam's final fling was the non-stop haul, by *Flying Scotsman* itself, to commemorate the 40th anniversary of the inauguration of that service Happily the train's great name lives on.

THE FLYING SCOTSMAN

Peppercorn A1 Pacific No. 60142 "Edward Fletcher" leaving Waverley with the up Flying Scotsman – early 1950s

© John Robertson

THE CORONATION AND THE CORONATION SCOT

The Coronation of the new King, George VI, in May 1937 had given hope and an impetus to an economy that was in any case beginning to climb out of the profound depression of the mid-1930s. The two major companies, the LMS and the LNER, decided to upgrade their prestige express services to Scotland, buoyed by the fact that the Empire Exhibition, to be held in Glasgow throughout the summer of 1938, would attract much passenger traffic in the short term at least.

THE CORONATION

The LNER had captured the headlines in the mid 1930s with the speed exploits of such locomotives as *Silver Link* and *Silver Fox*. The East Coast company therefore sought to strengthen its advantage by building completely new stock for its King's Cross – Waverley run with a journey time of six hours, far better than any motorist could hope to achieve in normal conditions on pre-motorway roads.

The trains were opulent. Not only were the A4 class locomotives streamlined but so too was the rear observation car, places in which could be rented by the hour. This facility was basically for spring and summer only as passengers were unwilling to pay a supplement for a better view of the dark in winter if the coach had run. They would be comfortable enough where they were, in their pressure-ventilated carriages.

Much admired too was the grouping of the club armchairs in First Class into little alcoves of four, with swivel tables. The art deco elegance of the train is well captured in some of the superb railway posters of the time.

THE CORONATION SCOT

The LMS was faced with different problems on the West Coast route and responded differently. Five new streamlined Pacific locomotives were ordered for the run and initially the coaches were standard stock, although an improved version came into service in 1939. There had been hopes of meeting the six hour standard set by the rival line, but the West Coast route suffered from the regular occurrence of large junctions such as Crewe, Preston and Stafford where there were permanent speed restrictions and severe gradients beyond Lancaster at Shap and Beattock. When a trial run reached 114 mph near Crewe but nearly ended in derailment, the LMS wisely settled for a safer and sustainable 6½ hours for the journey between Euston and Glasgow Central.

If the Coronation Scot was not totally purpose built, it still was sufficiently luxurious to satisfy the most demanding. Even the Third Class Dining Car provided a four-course lunch for 3/6d (17.5p) while a shilling more on the Edinburgh line, Third Class again, would have purchased a five-course dinner.

The LMS did have one major propaganda triumph in the months before the war. One of the "Princess Coronation" class locomotives, No. 6229 *Duchess of Hamilton,* was given the name and number of the original No. 6220 *Coronation* and dispatched to the World Fair in New York. There and in Eastern America she hauled a train of specially built coaches. In 1942 the engine was sent back but the rolling stock was trapped in the USA for the duration.

The great trains of 1937 never regained their glory. By 1940 stations were feebly-lit vaults, trains were almost unlit internally, sleepers were reserved for VIPs, restaurant cars disappeared and the prestige trains were taken out of service. In place of the softly-lit dining cars came corridors crammed with slumped, exhausted Servicemen. Austerity ruled until the mid-1950s and when at last it receded, so too did the great days of steam.

THE CORONATION
Painted in garter blue below the waist and marlborough blue above, with stainless steel trim, the train included a 'beaver-tail' observation car.
© Ian Allan Library

THE CORONATION SCOT
Stanier Pacific No. 6222 " Queen Mary" leaving Euston in June 1938
© H L Overend/Colour-Rail

THE RACE TO THE COAST

The invention in the early nineteenth century of the steamship and the steam locomotive meant that for the first time man could travel at a speed quicker than that of the fastest horse. It became possible to live at some distance from the great industrial cities and that strange beast, the commuter, was born.

Intense competition for the Clyde Coast traffic really began about 1850 and was mainly confined to the south bank of the river. It is true that there was competition on the Balloch route for the Loch Lomond steamers but at an early stage the North British had sewn up the "coastal tred" as Neil Munro's Para Handy would have described it. By the mid-century the Lower Firth had been reached by the Glasgow Paisley & Greenock Railway and the Glasgow Paisley Kilmarnock & Ayr Railway. This last amalgamated with the Glasgow Dumfries & Carlisle Railway and several smaller lines to form the Glasgow & South Western in 1850.

By 1851 the Caledonian Railway had absorbed the Glasgow Paisley & Greenock and was running services to Greenock. The station, situated in Cathcart Street, was quite a distance from the pierhead but that did not matter since it would be another 20 years almost before the Glasgow & South Western competed on the route. When they did, their Princes Pier station, at the end of the steep descent from Kilmacolm, was considerably handier for the river steamers than the Caley station.

The Caledonian Railway was not disposed to accept this state of affairs and by 1889 had completed a three mile extension to Gourock which was both costly and difficult to build, involving as it did the construction of the Newton Street tunnel, the longest in Scotland at one mile 350 yards. At the same time the subsidiary Caledonian Steam Packet Company was formed (1888) after several previously unsuccessful efforts to supply a railway steamer service. The NB (after 1902) and GSWR did not use the device of a subsidiary company for their steamers but employed them directly.

Clearly, one could travel faster on land than on water and this prompted the Caledonian's next move, the doubling of the track between Greenock and Wemyss Bay, some eight miles further down the Clyde. This had originally been built by the Greenock & Wemyss Bay Railway although operated by the Caledonian since its inception. Whoever had Wemyss Bay controlled effectively the bulk of the Rothesay and Millport trade and in 1904 the line was graced by a terminal station which could claim to be the most elegant in Scotland. Wemyss Bay station with its delicate arches, floral hanging baskets and round central office, provides the back cover to this book. Between trains it was and is cathedral-like. When the boat trains arrived there was a thunderous roar as hundreds of feet raced down the long covered wooden-floored corridors for the steamers. Such was the premium on speed that some of these trains were "no-luggage" trains, that is, the steamer sailed without waiting for the transfer of luggage. The paddles would be churning the sea to a froth within seven minutes of the train drawing in.

Forty-five minutes took the passenger from Glasgow Central to Gourock, the crack trains stopping only at Paisley. The line from Central was the preserve of the Caley Coast Bogies and 4-4-0s also worked the hilly St Enoch–Princes Pier line. Tank engines appeared on services in LMS days.

So reliable were the steamers and trains (only river fog offered a real hazard) that until 1939 people regularly commuted to Glasgow from the remote Argyllshire village of Tighnabruaich in the Kyles of Bute.

Of course there was expensive duplication pre-1914, two stations at Ardrossan for the Arran traffic for instance, but for the traveller it was an exceptional service. In the glory days of 1890–1910 there were regular evening and late-night cruises to see the Largs and Millport illuminations and to visit the Rothesay Entertainers and Sunday trains (though not to Princes Pier) proliferated as the excessively grim Sabbatarianism weakened.

The most dramatic changes came after 1945. The paddle steamers survived until the early 1960s then vanished almost totally for cruise purposes. The car ferries which took their place were invaluable for residents and death for trippers, being claustrophobic and uncomfortable. Visitors who had cars wished to go further afield.

By 1959 Princes Pier had gone as a regular passenger station, Clyde steamers no longer called there and people now flew the Atlantic rather than go by the great CPR Empresses. It was too costly to pay steamer crews to work until almost midnight and the unions would have opposed it anyway. The elegance of the silver service in the dining saloons had been replaced by paper cups and formica.

The commuter and to a degree the holiday traffic survive. It had been a wonderful buccaneering episode in the history of Scottish railways and its legacy has been beautiful locomotives, beautiful ships and one outstandingly beautiful station.

WEMYSS BAY PIER

TS Queen Mary II leaving the pier – 1973

© Dugald Cameron

CALEDONIAN RAILWAY No. 123
'THE CALEY SINGLE'

The story of Caledonian Railway No. 123 is a remarkable one. Built by Neilson & Company for show at the Edinburgh International Exhibition of 1886 the engine with a highly unusual wheel arrangement of 4-2-2 for a Scottish railway won a gold medal and equally golden opinions when put to work for the Caledonian Railway.

Right from the outset in July 1888, this single-wheeler product of the Hydepark Works was pitched into the Great Race North between the West and East coast lines from London. This had its origin in the decision to make the Scotch Express, as the East Coast train was first known, available to all three classes of passenger, thereby creaming off a large section of the third-class traffic from its West Coast rival. As a result of the race times came down from 9 hours to Edinburgh on the East Coast line and 10 on the West to 8¼ and 8½ respectively.

No. 123 was assigned exclusive rights to the Carlisle–Edinburgh section of the West Coast journey. In this capacity as sole racer she put up some homeric performances.

The distance from Carlisle to Edinburgh was fractionally over 100 miles but with two stiff gradients to surmount, as there was the climb to Beattock at 1014 feet and then between Carstairs and Edinburgh the line reached almost 900 feet at Cobbinshaw.

On this most testing of assignments No. 123 regularly averaged 56 mph or better and on one occasion on 9 August 1888 the 100·6 miles was covered in 102 minutes 33 seconds with the normal racing train of four coaches.

When its racing days were over, No. 123 became the engine which hauled the Directors' Inspection Coach before being assigned to work the Tayside route between Perth and Dundee. In this role and re-numbered post-1923 as LMS No. 14010 and painted maroon it was the last single-wheeler in Great Britain to be engaged in normal service when it was withdrawn in 1935.

On its retiral in 1935 it was repainted in the bright blue Caledonian livery. Following another overhaul in 1957 No. 123 emerged to pull special trains for enthusiasts and performed magnificently even in the dreadful winter of 1963 on the exposed Callander & Oban line. Like the Highland Railway No. 103 it was presented to the Museum of Transport in Glasgow by the British Railways Board in 1966.

It's a fact –

The largest class of locomotive ever built in Scotland for a Scottish railway was Dugald Drummond's '294' class for the Caledonian Railway, better known as the Caley 'Jumbos'. Built from 1883 to 1898 these 0-6-0 tender engines were 'maids of all work', some being goods locos and some passenger ones. The class eventually numbered 244 engines and some survived to record 80 years in service.

A TIGHT SCHEDULE

The order from the Caledonian Railway Company, dated 23 January 1886, allowed only 67 days for the building of No. 123 which was to be displayed at the Edinburgh International Exhibition in April

© Mitchell Library, Glasgow

APPROACHING CALLANDER

Caledonian Railway No 123 with the two preserved Caley coaches on an excursion to Callander in October 1964

© Dugald Cameron

NORTH BRITISH RAILWAY No. 673
"MAUDE"

The story of *Maude* is one of an apparently humdrum goods engine which seemed destined for an unglamorous if useful working life, but through force of circumstance became very celebrated in its latter years.

Maude started life as a North British Railway class 'C' 0-6-0 goods engine built at Neilson's in 1891 to a Matthew Holmes design, one of that engineer's "18-inchers" , as they were known.

Under the modest anonymity of No. 673 the sturdy little engine worked at various depots in Central Scotland. The engine underwent the customary updating processes, most notably in 1915 when a protective cab at last gave crews some worthwhile protection against the Scottish winter and, not infrequently, the Scottish summer.

By that time however, war was raging in France and in 1917 25 of these engines were commandeered by the Railway Operating Division for service in that theatre of war. It would be two more years before they were released to return to civilian service and, as a recognition of the valuable contribution they had made, all 25 of this class were given names of military leaders and places of prominent battles, No. 673 being one of those so honoured.

Titles conferred included *Foch, Petain, Allenby, Haig* and even Bruce Bairnsfather's immortal old sweat, *Ole Bill*.

No. 673 was awarded the name of a man who had earned fame in another theatre of war. Lieutenant General Sir Frederick Stanley Maude KCB had been appointed to command the allied forces in Mesopotamia (Iraq) after the disastrous surrender at Kut-al-Amara. He re-invigorated the British effort and was prominent in the re-capture of Baghdad, unfortunately dying almost immediately afterwards of cholera as a result of drinking infected milk.

The locomotive came home, bearing its new title and returned to a quiet existence of working goods trains out of Haymarket. On re-grouping in 1923 it became LNER No. 9673 and its home was Haymarket until 1964 when it spent the last two years of its official working life at Bathgate.

The Scottish Railway Preservation Society had long had its collective eye on *Maude* and after much re-fitting and a certain amount of cannibalisation it began to pull passenger trains for the Society in 1967.

Since then the career of *Maude* has become much more glamorous, rather like a douce housewife who becomes a cabaret singer in her late fifties. The locomotive has appeared in several films and under her own steam went down to Liverpool to take part in the Rocket 150 Years celebrations. She has steamed to Inverness and gone back to old haunts by taking "Santa Specials" round the Edinburgh Suburban Circle.

In 1992 *Maude* celebrated her centenary a trifle late, the tardy celebration being caused by the fact that for two years she had been undergoing a major overhaul. In November 1992 she returned to her home at the Bo'ness and Kinneil Railway where the popularity of this delightful veteran remains absolutely undiminished.

N.B. No. 673

"Maude" hauls a train along the foreshore at Bo'ness en route to Birkhill on the Bo'ness & Kinneil Railway – October 1993

HIGHLAND RAILWAY No. 103
THE JONES GOODS

The Highland Railway may have been one of the more remote British rail networks but in the matter of locomotives it was in the forefront of developments. When David Jones then Superintendent of the Highland Railway decided in 1894 to move to a 4-6-0 he placed an order with Sharp Stewart, not for a cautious trial horse, but for fifteen of them. His boldness was rewarded, the new locomotives were a success from the outset. No. 103 was the first of the class and therefore the first 4-6-0 to work in Britain. The belated appearance is worthy of comment because for years British manufacturers had been making locomotives with this wheel arrangement for the world market.

The Jones "Big Goods" as they were sometimes known were powerful and distinctive presences with their louvred or slotted chimneys and were designed to haul heavy goods trains. For the bulk of its working life No. 103 served on the Perth – Inverness – Wick – Thurso line. On the grouping of 1923 the new number allocated was 17916 and under the LMS the engine continued to work until eventually withdrawn in 1934.

At this stage, by a most fortunate decision of the LMS she was ear-marked for preservation and was repainted to this end in the original Highland Railway olive green. She was kept at St Rollox for 25 years and then, in 1959, readied for the hauling of special trains as the approaching withdrawal of steam engines from regular main line working made them all the more highly regarded. No. 103 appeared on excursions to the Kelvin Hall for the Scottish Industries Exhibition in 1959.

Again there was a change of raiment, this time to the Brighton yellow or "improved engine green" of William Stroudley which had been used on the Highland Railway in the early days when Stroudley had been Locomotive Superintendent between 1865–69 before moving to the London Brighton & South Coast Railway. Like many another re-furbishing, there is some doubt as to whether No. 103 had ever been so arrayed in her working life. A substantial body of opinion thinks not.

In her new role she was a great success hauling excursion trains and there was one memorable televised run pulling a mixed train from Kyle of Lochalsh to Dingwall in June 1960. In 1966 the engine was given by the British Railways Board to the Museum of Transport in Glasgow.

It's a fact –

Scotland's first railway was the Tranent – Cockenzie Wagonway, about 16km (10 miles) east of Edinburgh, laid down with wooden rails in 1722. Part of the line was used on 21 September 1745 in the course of the Battle of Prestonpans with the Young Pretender, Prince Charles Edward. Iron rails were used from 1815. It continued as a horse tramway until after 1880 when part was converted into a steam colliery railway.

THE JONES GOODS

Highland Railway No. 103 is replenished at Dumfries shed while running on an excursion in G&SWR territory – 1965

© Alan Carlaw

THE CALEDONIAN RAILWAY DUNALASTAIRS

It was the fashion of railway directors and management in the last century to immortalise themselves in the naming of engine stock. Thus the title, *Dunalastair*, redolent of centuries of Highland chiefdom, was in fact taken from the Perthshire estate of the then chairman of the Caledonian Railway, J C Bunten as later the name *Cardean* would also perpetuate an official's estate in the country.

The *Dunalastair* class marked the beginning of the shift towards large-boilered locomotives and although small by latter-day standards, these 4-4-0s were both pleasing to look upon and highly effective over both short and long hauls.

They first appeared, fifteen in number, in 1896 and at once made an immense impact. In all 87 locomotives were built in five distinct groupings and they were immediately placed on the Carlisle runs. When superheated engines were introduced with the fifth class of *Dunalastairs* in 1910, big economies in coal and water resulted.

On the Carlisle – Perth run a superheater could do the return trip on between 4 and 4½ tons of coal. One of the kenspeckle firemen of the period, Jock McLeish, tells how the quantity of coal required for the trip almost doubled when using a non-superheated engine. On reaching Carlisle they needed more coal for the return trip and the driver, Cuddy Mitchell, supervised the loading at Carlisle. He demanded box after box of coal from the coalman, until, at length, he pronounced himself satisfied. The coalman, exasperated beyond endurance, shouted "Back a bit!" and then "Stop". Cuddy Mitchell enquired "what was up?" to receive the aggrieved reply "Take a box down the bloody lum and you'll maybe have enough!"

The *Dunalastairs* proved their worth over sprint distances too. They became celebrated as the "Gourock Flyers" at a time when steamer competition on the Firth of Clyde was at its peak and the Caley and the Glasgow & South-Western Railways were shaving seconds off their times from Glasgow to the coast. The *Dunalastair II* class of engine returned some remarkable times on the down-river journey. The 4.08 pm from the Central covered the distance of just over 26 miles in 32 minutes and there were notorious sharp curves over the last six miles or so of the line. In later years the 4.13 pm did the journey in 35 minutes.

Much has been made of the blue livery of the Caledonian engines and of these *Dunalastairs* of J F McIntosh in particular. In fact the Caledonian blue varied over the years. Originally a Prussian blue, the shade had lightened to almost sky-blue by the time the *Dunalastair IVs* had commenced service. The engines were a delight to behold with various parts, including steps and buffer beams, picked out in crimson lake. Subsequently five engines were built by Neilsons for Belgian State Railways where there were altogether more than 200 locomotives of similar design.

J F McIntosh retired in 1914 three years after he had been appointed CVO by King George V in recognition of his services to Royal railway travel over two reigns.

It's a fact –
The first 'proper' railway in Scotland was the Kilmarnock & Troon Railway, incorporated on 27 May 1808 and opened for horse-drawn traffic on 6 July 1812. Steam traction was introduced in 1817.

THE FIRST DUNALASTAIR
Caledonian Railway No. 721 posed in classic style by proud enginemen – the coupling rod had to be down – at Carstairs in 1919
© A E Glen

GLASGOW & SOUTH WESTERN RAILWAY No. 394
"LORD GLENARTHUR"

This particular engine was not aristocratic in origin starting out life as No. 11 of the Glasgow & South Western Railway, and having been built at the company workshops in Kilmarnock in 1897. This of itself was unusual since the G&SWR rarely produced more than one locomotive per year in its latter days, their town neighbours, Andrew Barclay Sons & Co being much more prolific.

No. 11 was of great interest to railway enthusiasts as it was reckoned to be the first four cylinder 4-4-0 engine in Britain, and an innovative piece of work by James Manson. It dwarfed most of the other engines on the line but was thought to be heavy on fuel and underwent two major transformations. The first of these was in 1915 when it was re-boilered with apparently beneficial results for economy and the second was in 1922 when it had not so much a refit as a total rebuild. In the words of a contemporary writer "only the wheels were original". It was renumbered No. 394 in 1919.

At 6' 9½" the wheels were remarkable enough in all conscience and worthy of the title now conferred upon the locomotive of *Lord Glenarthur*, in honour of the last chairman of the G&SW. The latter had less than a year to run as an independent organisation before the grouping of 1923. No. 394 was the first company engine to be dignified by a name in 65 years, the previous one having been the 2-4-0 *Galloway* in 1857.

In January 1923 *Lord Glenarthur* worked the Ayr – Glasgow route. It was dwarfed by the giant 4-6-4 tank engines which did much of the day to day work but it performed creditably without winning universal approbation. There were lukewarm comments:- "Did some useful work", "serviceable but hardly a masterpiece."

Nevertheless, *Lord Glenarthur* worked this section until 1929 when it became a spare engine. In 1931 it was sent to Girvan where it worked chiefly on the "Paddy" train between Stranraer and Ayr although occasionally it broke new ground when hauling an excursion to Portpatrick and more improbably, returning an Ayr excursion to Alloa.

When it had re-emerged in 1925 from a visit to the workshops it had been reclad in LMS red and bore the number 14509. Its last years were a gentle slide towards oblivion. By 1933 it was on the sleepy backwater of the Dalmellington–Rankinston line in South Ayrshire and in 1934 the great engine, with its distinctive Robert Whitelegg cab, was finally withdrawn from service.

It's a fact –

The highest station on the British Rail network is at Corrour on the West Highland line from Glasgow to Fort William. Situated 94.7 miles from Glasgow it is 1,347 feet above sea-level. Until its closure in May 1965, the highest station was Dalnaspidal, 51 miles north of Perth on the former Highland Railway main line from Perth to Inverness, at 1,420 feet above sea-level.

PLATFORM 2, ST ENOCH STATION
Waiting for the signal, the Sou' West's "Lord Glenarthur" prepares to leave with a train for Ayr – 1923
© A E Glen

CALEDONIAN RAILWAY No. 903
"CARDEAN"

The success of the *Dunalastair* class of locomotive gave rise for a demand for heavier, more powerful engines to haul the corridor trains and sleeping-car trains that were now becoming common place in the last decade of the nineteenth century. This demand was to be satisfied in quality, if not in quantity, by the *Cardean* class of the Caledonian Railway. Only the first, No. 903, *Cardean* bore a name as opposed to a number and the title was taken from the name of the estate of the then Deputy Chairman, Edward Cox. This locomotive became legendary.

The presiding genius in their construction was John Farquharson McIntosh who, in their design, combined size, strength and beauty. They were half as heavy again as the *Dunalastair I* class but there was nothing ponderous in their appearance. McIntosh himself was scarcely an aesthete in looks. More of a one-armed roustabout in many ways, he was greatly valued by King Edward VII as an unending source of smutty stories and he was often summoned to the presence on the Royal Trains of the time.

The huge engines were allotted specific tasks. No. 903 *Cardean* ran the "The Corridor" to Carlisle almost every day for ten years, leaving Glasgow Central at 2 pm and returning in the evening with the corresponding Euston train which it picked up at Carlisle.

Drivers and engines were fixed allocations too and the celebrated David Gibson had charge of the engine every day between 1911 and 1916. Under his gimlet eye and nervous cosseting, the great engine ran in massive glory and with the regularity of a metronome. No housewife ever lavished more care on a piece of household equipment.

An elderly cousin of mine bears this out. Coming north from Liverpool to Glasgow as a child just before the grouping of 1923, he was astonished at the light blue livery of the engine which would transport him. He was told he could pat it by the driver, and did. Going back to his carriage, he turned a few yards down the platform to see the driver, on the platform by now, wiping away the paw-prints with a rag.

Cardean was built in 1906 at St Rollox and in her time ran non-stop from Glasgow to Carlisle. The home depot was Polmadie in Glasgow and the engine survived a nasty mishap when near Crawford on 2 April 1909, she broke a crank axle and was almost derailed.

A few years later and a few miles further south, one of her sisters, No. 907, was in the worst British rail accident of all time, the Quintinshill disaster, and was so badly damaged as to be unfit for further service.

After the grouping of 1923 *Cardean* remustered as No. 14752 of the LMS and served her new masters well until 1930. Well into the autumn of her days she could haul a load of more than 300 tons up Beattock summit without assistance.

She had the lovely deep-toned whistle which had something of the resonance of a steam-boat. The standard Caley hooter was adopted for the LMS by Sir William Stanier. No more graceful 4-6-0s ever took to the rails and the *Cardean* class exemplified the very best of the pre-1914 British steam locomotive.

GLASGOW CENTRAL STATION – 1908

Caledonian Railway No. 903 "Cardean" prepares to leave platform 2 on 'The Corridor' – the engine so polished that you could see your face in it!

NORTH BRITISH RAILWAY No. 875
"MIDLOTHIAN"

Normally when a locomotive is the subject of a preservation order it is lovingly restored to former glory (sometimes to glory it never had formerly) and becomes an object of veneration either in a museum or as a hauler of special trains on great occasions. The story of *Midlothian* could best be described as a preservation venture that did not quite come off.

Midlothian was one of the North British 4-4-2 Class H locomotives which were the brainchild of W Reid and which were designed with the Edinburgh–Carlisle 'Waverley' line very much in mind. For some time the North British Railway had been searching for an adequate reply to the 4-6-0s of the two other major Scottish railways operating in the Lowlands, the Caledonian and the Glasgow & South Western, and Reid had supplied the solution with these mighty new engines.

Midlothian emerged from the Hyde Park works of the North British Locomotive Company in August 1906 and initially operated from St Margaret's sheds in Edinburgh between that city and Carlisle before assuming the Aberdeen run and transferring to the Haymarket depot.

The middle part of its career was fairly orthodox, as after the Armistice in 1918 the engine was assigned to the Edinburgh–Dundee line while in 1920 a superheated boiler was installed by Robert Stephenson's. The grouping of 1923 saw the allocation of a new LNER number, 9875.

Service on the Edinburgh–Glasgow line followed and a return to the shed of her salad days, St Margaret's. In December 1937 *Midlothian* was withdrawn from service and a useful and blameless life seemed to be at a close.

Events proved otherwise. There was a trickle of correspondence in *The Scotsman*, by no means a flood of indignation, which suggested that since Highland Railway No.103 and Caledonian Railway No.123 had already been saved from the breakers, perhaps an Atlantic could also be kept for posterity in the hope that this might form the kernel of a subsequent Scottish Railway Museum.

One or two of the correspondents muttered gloomily that they had heard that there would be no more locomotives built in Scotland anyway.

Amazingly this tepid appeal reached the ears of the LNER company's chairman, William Whitelaw, and the Chief Mechanical Engineer, Sir Nigel Gresley. They ordered a stay of execution.

There was one major problem. Execution had, so to speak, already started and the engine was in the process of being dismembered at Cowlairs. The result was not so much a restoration as a reconstruction, with parts from other engines being commandeered. In this new guise *Midlothian* wrung another couple of summers out of life, a popular figure in the apple-green livery which denoted the special status of LNER passenger engines.

The outbreak of war in September 1939 saw the end of *Midlothian*. Survival rather than preservation was the overwhelming priority of the railways for the next six years and the good publicity that might have accrued had vanished in the cross-fire of the censor's pencil and the reduction in newspaper size. Breaking-up commenced in November 1939 and this time there was no reprieve. With a mileage standing at 1,408,823 *Midlothian* had fairly paid its dues.

EASTFIELD EVENING

"Midlothian" has been coaled, watered and turned for yet another roster in LNER service – 1933

© A E Glen

CALEDONIAN RAILWAY No. 419

This humdrum description conceals the identity of the last survivor of the last class of tank engine that the Caledonian Railway built. It was known as the 439 class and was built to the design of the celebrated J F McIntosh.

The tanks were the Marthas of the railway world, destined for service on the Glasgow and Edinburgh suburban lines, in the days when the capital boasted a respectable suburban network, or to work the picturesque branch lines such as Forfar – Brechin, Connel Ferry – Ballachulish, or in LMS days Ballinluig – Aberfeldy.

No. 419 emerged from St Rollox works in 1907 and was at first set to work on the Glasgow suburban services. Here, especially on the Cathcart Circle, the 439s were replacing the 104 class which was known as the Cathcart Circle class. The feature of these was the very small driving wheels (4' 6" as against the 5' 9" of the new arrivals) to take account of the short distances between stations, less than a mile in some instances. The small wheels were to improve acceleration on leaving stations and the distinctive appearance of these engines gave rise to their nickname of "The Threepenny Bits."

Sometimes the sturdy '439' tanks were allowed to rub shoulders, literally, with the aristocracy of the line. No. 419 served a spell at Beattock in the 1920s where the main duty was to bank the heavy trains from the south a distance of ten miles from Beattock station to the signal box at Beattock summit, after which with a self-conscious friskiness the banking engine would return backwards or "bunker-first" down the line.

With the grouping in 1923 came a re-numbering to LMS No. 15189 and a posting to Ardrossan which was short-lived. Dalry Road in Edinburgh beckoned and for the next thirty years No. 419 was a familiar sight to Edinburgh suburban rail travellers. When the railways were nationalised in 1948 the number changed to 55189 and under that number she was in at the closure of the Barnton line in 1951.

There was now less need for tank engines in the east and the new depot was Polmadie where tasks included the moving of empty passenger coaches and a return to the Cathcart Circle. The last years were spent at Carstairs where its working career ended in 1962.

The then recently formed Scottish Railway Preservation Society was eager to acquire a Caley tank engine. It had its sights on No. 55124 but it proved too far gone to be a fit candidate. Thus No. 55189 became the new target. It was purchased from British Railways for £750, an individual donation coming from Mr W E C Watkinson of Worcestershire, who also provided £500 to restore the engine to its original Caledonian livery. The rejected No. 55124 still had a contribution to make for she was fitted with an original Caledonian chimney and this was transferred to the SRPS's new acquisition in place of the stovepipe chimney she bore and which so offended traditionalists.

The restoration gave rise to some debate. There were animated discussions on whether McIntosh's original blue might well have been lighter. This did not matter. The Society had its first engine and, to mix metaphors, its flagship.

As locomotives in these circumstances do, it began a round of "personal appearances." In 1975 it took part in the celebrations to mark the 150th anniversary of the Stockton & Darlington Railway and seven years later it went even further – though not under its own steam – when it figured in the centenary programme of the Bluebell Railway in Sussex.

Back home at Bo'ness it was ever-popular for short excursions and was chosen to open the extension of the Bo'ness & Kinneil Railway to Birkhill in 1989. At present No. 419 awaits an extensive overhaul.

As a class the 439 tank engines were reliable and hard-working. Most of them gave up the ghost only when maintenance was abandoned in the last days of steam. Of all engines I have a special affection for them for they were part of my daily life for the better part of a decade.

A GRAND WEE ENGINE

The versatile Caley 0-4-4 tank No. 419 heads a train for Birkhill on the Bo'ness & Kinneil Railway in 1989

© Ann Glen

NORTH BRITISH RAILWAY No. 256
"GLEN DOUGLAS"

Built in the Cowlairs works of the North British Railway Company for service with that Company – as indeed was every engine in this class – *Glen Douglas* began its career in 1913, just before the outbreak of the First World War. Although it served throughout the NB empire it was to be indelibly associated with the West Highland line. All the engines of this class were named after glens either adjacent to or associated with the West Highland Line hence the appearance of such engines as *Glen Sloy, Glen Fruin* and *Glen Ogle.*

These 4-4-0 engines, superheated and built to the design of William P Reid were to prove invaluable on the taxing and twisting West Highland Line with its heavily graded routes, their small wheels giving good adhesion.

In particular they performed well in tandem during the Second World War when the fall-off in tourist traffic was more than compensated for by the large numbers of naval personnel and the transport of troops to the Commando-training area at Spean Bridge.

In its latter days *Glen Douglas,* originally numbered NBR 256 but through various transmutations No. 62469 under British Railways was the only locomotive of its class to work out of Keith, most of the sister locomotives in the north were based on Kittybrewster. In late years *Glen Douglas* was often to be found pulling goods trains on the Deeside or Elgin line, far from her native North British haunts. The engine was an imposing sight at almost 57 feet long and weighing 103 tons in full working order.

Glen Douglas was not retired until 1959 when she was restored to North British livery and adopted once more her original number of 256. For a brief spell she continued to work special trains but by 1966 she was a prized exhibit in the Glasgow Transport Museum.

No amount of exhibition can compensate for the inability to steam and there was great joy when the Glasgow District Council Arts and Culture Committee agreed to ScotRail's proposal that the locomotive could be restored to full working order at Bo'ness.

Hopefully the locomotive will undergo a thorough renovation at Bo'ness and will soon be returned to the West Highland Line to revive memories for those who were fortunate enough to see her surge up testing inclines apparently effortlessly. As a traveller from those days has written:- " To travel in a long train of 11 or 12 coaches hauled by a pair of *Glens* was an experience never to be forgotten".

It's a fact –
The largest masonry arch railway bridge in Britain is the central span of the Ballochmyle Viaduct over the River Ayr on the Glasgow & South Western main line from Glasgow to Carlisle. It was begun in March 1846 and finished in March 1848. The arch has a semicircular span of 55m (181 feet), *c.* 30 cm longer than the Wiesen Bridge in Switzerland. It carries the line 51.5 m (169ft) above the river bed and is now the highest railway bridge in Great Britain.

GLEN DOUGLAS

Once again in North British livery, No. 256 is seen here on a special excursion in Fife in 1960

© A E Glen

GREAT NORTH of SCOTLAND RAILWAY No. 49
"GORDON HIGHLANDER"

Gordon Highlander or "The Sodjer" as it was more generally and affectionately known was ordered by the Great North of Scotland Railway from the Hyde Park works of the North British Locomotive Company as a replacement for engines which had been worked into the ground in the course of the First World War.

Others of this class were built at the GNSR's own workshops at Inverurie, near Aberdeen and in essence these engines were a superheated version of the William Pickersgill locomotives built before the war although by the time *Gordon Highlander* was built T E Heywood had become that line's Locomotive Superintendent.

"The Sodjer" had a troubled start. The coal strike of 1921 led to an ugly-looking and only partially successful experiment with oil-burning. As things got back to normal the engine was allocated to the runs between Aberdeen, Keith and Elgin. In 1923 the LNER took over its management and it was re-numbered from 49 to 6849 and painted apple green.

For much of its career *Gordon Highlander's* home shed was Kittybrewster but as newer and more powerful locomotives came north the "The Sodjer" increasingly operated from Fraserburgh on the celebrated Buchan branch line.

There were high days and holidays too for occasionally in conjunction with another 'D40', as the locomotives had been re-classified, *Gordon Highlander* would be chosen to take the Royal Train from Aberdeen to Ballater. This indirectly assured that maintenance of the engine would always be at top level.

As its running career drew peacefully to a close in the 1950s the engine was most often to be seen on the Speyside line which connected Craigellachie and Boat of Garten. It was retired in June 1958 and almost immediately re-clad in the vivid green GNSR livery which had never actually adorned her in her working life.

Gordon Highlander now came south and spent some time at Dawsholm shed in Glasgow. From here she made special excursion trips over tracks of the Scottish railways and proved very popular with the public in general and rail enthusiasts in particular.

'The Sodjer' was bequeathed to the Glasgow Transport Museum by the British Railways Board in 1966 and remains there to this day. Those who go to look at her may feel a sense of railway history if they reflect that they are admiring the last GNSR locomotive ever to have been in active service.

It's a fact –
The highest summit on British Rail is at Druimuachdar, 452 m (1484 ft), between Dalnaspidal and Dalwhinnie on the former Highland Railway main line from Perth to Inverness. In 1902 a 11.7 km (7.3 mile) branch was opened from the Caledonian Railway's Glasgow – Carlisle main line at Elvanfoot to Wanlockhead, the highest village in Scotland. The station was at a height of 431 m (1413 ft) but the line climbed to 456 m (1498 ft). It closed on 2 January 1939.

"THE SODJER"

Far from Great North of Scotland tracks, No. 49 "Gordon Highlander" prepares to leave Glasgow Queen Street Station with a special excursion in 1960

© A E Glen

LONDON & NORTH EASTERN RAILWAY No. 4472
"FLYING SCOTSMAN"

It is probably true to say that this is the best-known locomotive in the history of British railways, *Rocket* being the only possible exception. For years any pacey Scottish wing three-quarter or outstanding sprinter could be sure of having the title *Flying Scotsman* conferred upon him.

Built in Doncaster, *Flying Scotsman* was the subject of re-numbering, owing to the grouping of 1923. The unstreamlined Gresley Pacific started as No. 1472 on what had been the Great Northern Railway but before coming into service it had become No. 4472 on the LNER.

Right from the start the giant 4-6-2 caught the public attention and it was chosen to represent the company at the Wembley Exhibition of 1924, undergoing additional ornamentation in the thought that it would be used to pull Royal trains.

Early in its career, in 1928, *Flying Scotsman* became involved in the so-called Race to the North which had recently been very publicly if very spuriously revived. Because minimum time schedules had been agreed between the LNER and LMS the rivalry was confined to the length of non-stop segments of the route. In the case of the Scotsman the undertaking was King's Cross to Edinburgh non-stop in 8¼ hours. On 30 November 1934 the locomotive recorded the first authenticated speed of 100 mph in British railway history. Some notion of the physically demanding life of the footplate man can be gathered from the fact that Fireman Webster shovelled nine tons of coal in that single day's work.

The great engine would remain in service for another 29 years before being withdrawn in January 1963 and bought by Mr Alan Pegler. For a few years it was the only steam locomotive permitted to use BR tracks and it made history when, 45 years old and 40 years to the day, it performed the last steam journey between King's Cross and Waverley on 1 May 1968.

After this triumph the next few years were chequered. In 1969 a reasonably successful tour of the United States and Canada was made but the engine was then out of circulation for a year. A visit to British Week at the San Francisco Fair of 1972 was a dismal failure and there was a real chance that the debt-ridden locomotive would be sold off across the Atlantic.

The saviour was the Hon W H McAlpine who arranged for the locomotive to be transported back to Britain. The voyage on the *California Star* was extremely stormy but safely accomplished.

In the early 1970s the giant engine, often with two tenders in tow as water points were becoming scarce, was operating on the Torbay Railway in the West Country. It was allowed to take excursion trips over certain authorised routes and was a proud participant in the 150th anniversary celebrations of the Stockton & Darlington Railway which were held in 1975. Many railway accolades have fallen to No. 4472 which has participated in the Centennial events in Australia even reaching Alice Springs in 1989.

During 1993 the locomotive was restored to its final British Railways condition as No. 60103 with double blastpipe and Kylchap double chimney, German type smoke deflectors and Brunswick green livery.

It's a fact –
The longest railway tunnel in Scotland is at Greenock on the former Caledonian Railway from Glasgow to Gourock. At 1920 m (1 mile 340 yards) it was opened on 1 June 1889.

"FLYING SCOTSMAN"

On a rare visit to Scotland No. 4472 called at Ayr in 1983 for the Rail Fair at the ScotRail depot

© Ann Glen

LONDON MIDLAND & SCOTTISH RAILWAY No. 6100
"ROYAL SCOT"

Shortly after the grouping of 1923 the LMS had to confront the disagreeable fact that it was seriously deficient in the possession of strong express passenger locomotives.

Under pressure it might have conceded that the Gresley Pacifics of the LNER were more modern but when it borrowed *Launceston Castle* from the Great Western Railway to work the Euston–Crewe run for a month and it comfortably outperformed the home stable, the extent of the LMS inferiority became horrifyingly apparent. (In 1925 the LNER Pacific was also proved to be no better than any LMS motive power.)

Accordingly in 1926 the NB Loco Works in Glasgow were asked to build 50 4-6-0 three-cylinder engines. Constraints of time meant that the order was split between the Hyde Park works and the Queen's Park works (formerly those of Dübs) on the south side of the city.

Initially only the first of the class, No. 6100, was named, taking the title which distinguished the class as a whole. There were some who contend that the naming of the first 25 of the 50 engines after regiments, or more properly individual soldiers since the names *Irish Guardsman* and *Royal Dragoon* occurred, was an afterthought. These writers would argue that the locomotive *Royal Scot* took its name from the train service rather than from the historic First Regiment of Foot. Be that as it may, the second 25 were called after famous early locomotives such as *Lancashire Witch* and *Fury*.

The locomotives of the Royal Scot class took over the Euston-Glasgow Central run in September 1927 but unfortunately were hard put to maintain times. The naming system had proved attractive, regiments vied with each other to submit ornamental crests while outline engravings of the old and famous engines were similarly displayed.

Royal Scot itself, No. 6100, was selected to make a tour of the United States in 1933 which would include the World's Fair at Chicago. Even here there is some doubt for a school of thought has it that another Derby-built locomotive was re-numbered 6100 for the purposes of the trip. At any rate a "Royal Scot" had to be equipped with the large electric front lamp, bell and the cowcatcher which were obligatory for running in the United States. It steamed over 11,000 miles there and in Canada without requiring anything in the way of even minor repair. The same could not be said of the accompanying eight carriages which made up the train for they suffered severely at the hands of over-inquisitive souvenir hunters.

One of the strangest things about this class of engine was that all its members underwent so radical a rebuilding as to emerge from the process almost as new creations. Even stranger was the fact that much of this major surgery took place during the desperate war years of 1943 and 1944. This gave the class another generation of working life and the last four engines were only withdrawn from service in 1965. The locomotive with No. 6100 and the nameplate *Royal Scot* was purchased by Butlin's Holiday Camps and exhibited at Skegness. It is now at Bressingham in Norfolk as an exhibit.

The *Royal Scots* as a class performed splendidly on either side of the Second World War even if the titular head never quite managed to command the affection which was given to its more favoured East Coast rival.

"ROYAL SCOT"

Fowler 6P 4-6-0 No. 6100

© J F McEwan collection/Strathkelvin Libraries

LONDON MIDLAND & SCOTTISH RAILWAY No. 6399
"FURY"

It had seemed to most people that the Great Railway Race to the North had been won by the West Coast Line in the Inverness cape, deerstalker and shirtwaister days of 1895. The grouping of 1923 showed that ambitions in this direction had merely been dormant, not extinct and by 1928 the LNER gained a distinct psychological advantage with its daily non-stop run from King's Cross to Waverley, a feat which the West Coast Line could not emulate on a day to day basis.

The LNER Pacifics had much larger tenders with corridor connections to enable non-stop running to take place. Nevertheless the LMS decided to experiment with a high-pressure boiler on one of the new Royal Scot 4-6-0s.

Much of the pioneering work in this line had been done in Europe so that the boiler for this experiment was a joint venture between the Superheater Company (representing in Britain the great firm of Schmidt of Berlin) and the North British Locomotive Company itself. The engine so built was No. 6399 *Fury* and it was ready to be handed over by December 1929.

One or two minor problems had emerged during crew training but it was with optimism that the engine left Polmadie on the morning of 10 February 1930. The progress to Hamilton Palace Colliery Junction was slow and the driver informed his fireman and the representatives of both the Superheater Company and LMS Derby who were also in the cab that he was worried about the level of the water gauge in the closed circuit section of the boiler.

He was told that all was well but he had been right to be worried because at Carstairs there was a blow-back from the firebox. The driver scrambled out and returned to extinguish the fire but the fireman had sustained injuries and Mr Lewis Schofield, the Superheater representative, had received such severe burns that he died on the way to hospital.

Fury was towed back to Polmadie where intensive and protracted examination revealed a five-inch opening in one of the super-pressure tubes.

Too much pride was at stake to abandon the project at this stage and Fury was re-boilered. This refit and testing took another two years but when the engine re-emerged for fresh trials in late 1932 results were far from satisfactory.

In February 1933 Fury broke down while towing a truncated goods train near Wellingborough in Northamptonshire. A pilot engine had already been requisitioned because of falling pressure in the high pressure drum. Speeds had been poor and fuel consumption heavy and the LMS decided that enough was enough. The engine was rebuilt once more but this time renumbered as 6170 and given the name *British Legion*. So *Fury* passed from the scene, its main function having been to serve as a reminder that some experiments, by the very nature of the word, are not destined to succeed. The rebuild was an entirely conventional locomotive and remained in service until 1962.

"FURY"

LMS 6P 4-6-0 high-pressure locomotive No. 6399 in steam prior to entering service in 1929

LONDON & NORTH EASTERN RAILWAY No. 4488
"UNION OF SOUTH AFRICA"

In 1935 Edinburgh born Sir Nigel Gresley had caused a sensation with the introduction of his A4 class locomotives to coincide with the Silver Jubilee of King George V. *Union of South Africa*, originally planned to be named *Osprey*, was No.4488 and later No. 9 with the LNER, (No.60009 after re-muster to British Railways) came upon the scene slightly later in June 1937 by which time imperial fervour had taken another direction with the Coronation the previous month of George VI.

It was on the crest of this wave of sentiment that five locomotives, each bearing the name of an Empire country, were designated to pull the ultra-modern "Coronation" train between King's Cross and Waverley. *Union of South Africa* was an imposing, graceful machine with severe streamlining and carried the Union's springbok emblem on the side.

From its early days she was assigned to Haymarket shed and would spend almost a quarter of a century there before being transferred in May 1962 to Ferryhill, Aberdeen. In the course of that period she underwent several alterations, being double-chimneyed in 1958.

The locomotive combined the qualities of thoroughbred and workhorse to an astonishing degree. In the course of her career of 27 years she steamed an incredible 1,800,000 miles and after coming off the Waverley–King's Cross run she rendered consistent service hauling the three-hour "Bon Accord" between Aberdeen and Buchanan Street Glasgow.

Naturally there were milestones in a career so long and so accident-free. *Union of South Africa* was the last A4 to undergo a general repair at the Doncaster workshops and in 1964 she was the last A4 to take a train out of King's Cross.

She was withdrawn from general service in June 1966, just three months before the cessation of rostered steam services between Aberdeen and Glasgow. She was subsequently bought by Mr John Cameron for the Lochty Private Railway and remained operative in British Railways livery. Since then she has proved an enormous attraction whenever she has been made available to haul special trains. So enduring was she that in her career South Africa moved from being a pillar of the Empire to a country which cut off all ties with the Commonwealth, and all the while this most imposing and majestic of Scots-based locomotives ran giving great pleasure over the years to enthusiasts and linesiders alike.

It's a fact –
The Motherwell Signalling Centre near Glasgow was completed in 1973. It replaced 67 mechanical signal-boxes and one power box and now controls 200 km (124 miles) of route with 505 signals and 270 point machines, the largest control area in Britain. This includes 137 km (85 miles) of the main London – Glasgow line extending from Kirkpatrick, 19 km (12 miles) north of Carlisle to Cambuslang, 8 km(5 miles) south of Glasgow.

"NUMBER NINE"

Gresley A4 Pacific No. 60009 "Union of South Africa", with the "Elizabethan" headboard waits to return to Top shed – 1961

© Colour-Rail

BRITISH RAILWAYS No. 60532
"BLUE PETER"

Blue Peter was a Peppercorn A2 Class Pacific engine, the class taking its name from the Chief Mechanical Engineer of the LNER although he gave his name, Arthur H (reduced on the nameplate to A H) Peppercorn only to the prototype. The others were called after famous racehorses, so that *Blue Peter* has nothing to do with the popular children's television programme or indeed the pennant traditionally flown by departing vessels.

It was a distinguished enough equine name for the horse Blue Peter had recorded a notable double in 1939 by winning the 2000 Guineas and the Derby.

By the time *Blue Peter* was built renumbering of locomotives had taken place under British Railways and therefore it became No. 60532, instead of 532 which it would have been had it taken up duty for the LNER. *Blue Peter* was indeed the very first locomotive to experience this renumbering.

Initially one of these A2 type engines was allocated to Scotland but the number later increased to 11 as it was realised how suitable these 4-6-2s were for working lines north of the Border. Originally it had been envisaged that they would haul trains of between 500–600 tons at 60 mph but by the time they were ready for service the fashion had swung back towards lighter trains and *Blue Peter* and sister locomotives had always plenty of power in hand for the work they were called upon to do.

Blue Peter had rather a nomadic life being at various times assigned to Edinburgh, Aberdeen and Dundee. These engines did the bulk of their work on the Edinburgh–Aberdeen route although they not infrequently ran as far south as Newcastle and Carlisle.

In its time *Blue Peter* was serviced at Doncaster, Cowlairs, Darlington and Inverurie. The Peppercorns were very durable and hard-working, normally 90,000 miles were steamed between heavy repairs. The type persisted longer in Scotland, the last English-based A2 had gone by 1963 but it was 1966 before the final runs were made in Scotland.

Blue Peter was withdrawn in 1966 by which time it was Dundee-based and after a couple of years in store it was bought by Messrs G S Drury and J B Hollingsworth who formed the Blue Peter Locomotive Society. It was taken to Doncaster and painstakingly restored to its original apple green. It reverted to the LNER number of 532 which it had originally missed by a few weeks.

Recently the locomotive has been restored to full working order by the North Eastern Locomotive Preservation Group and, based at the North Yorkshire Moors Railway, has preserved the connection with Scotland by a special excursion visit. In the autumn of 1993 *Blue Peter* made a foray north to Dumfries, Kirkcaldy, Edinburgh Waverley, Stirling and Perth, allowing the locomotive's many Scottish admirers the chance once more to see a typical engine of the transitional period of the late 1940s when the four major companies became the nationalised British Railways.

It's a fact –
One of the world's oldest bridges still carrying a railway is that built in 1810 as an aqueduct to carry the Paisley & Johnstone Canal over the River Cart near Paisley. It was converted to a railway in 1885, becoming part of the Glasgow & South Western system.

"BLUE PETER"

Peppercorn A2 Pacific No. 60532 on a Special Train at Hawick on the Waverley Route – October 1966

GLASGOW QUEEN STREET STATION

Queen Street Station is comfortably the oldest of the four main Glasgow stations having set out in life in February 1842 as the western terminus of the Edinburgh & Glasgow Railway later to become the main Glasgow station of the North British Railway. It had, and still has, one of the most individual approaches of any British station in that the tracks, coming from the north, have to contend with a descent of almost exactly a mile through a tunnel, which was built at the insistence of the Port Dundas Canal Company, determined to make life as hard as possible for these new rivals.

The gradient of 1 in 42 made things difficult for arriving and departing trains. The latter were assisted on their way in the early days by ropes wound by a stationary engine while it was the beginning of the twentieth century before it was deemed safe to dispense with the incline brakes for arriving trains and allow them to come down the tunnel under their own brake power. When this decision was taken in 1908 the North British Railway commented, with praiseworthy Scots canniness, " While little or no saving would be affected, no additional expense would be involved". Just before this development tank engines were called in to boost trains up the incline, thus rendering the stationary engine and ropes redundant.

Today the station chiefly concerns itself with the Glasgow – Edinburgh route, one of the busiest lines in Britain, and one which links the two cities in 43 minutes while a second-string line between them operates from Glasgow Central which also sees the departure of the electrified line via Carstairs.

There was a time when East Coast trains for London left Queen Street, with some highly prestigious expresses among them, notably the *Queen of Scots*. The Helensburgh line was important too in the days of railway steamers since the North British fleet headquarters was at Craigendoran, just short of Helensburgh and the north-bank railway was the natural way for inhabitants of that section of the city to go "doon the watter". There they picked up one of the beautiful NB paddlers, bandbox-smart in red funnel, white band, black top and each bearing the name of a Walter Scott character.

Today Queen Street looks east and certainly north with services to Aberdeen, Dundee, Inverness and the West Highland Line, on which trains had an age-old penchant for leaving at 4.15 am or some such miniscule hour. In recent times the Balloch-Helensburgh-Airdrie commuter low-level line has fulfilled the same service that the Cathcart Circle has rendered on the opposite bank of the river.

There are seven high level platforms and two low level ones. The descent through the tunnel from Cowlairs has something of the voyage across the Styx about it. It is of course nothing like as sulphurous as in the days of steam but the yellow lights drifting past for what seems an eternity do serve to convey a disembodied feeling to the passenger.

The arriving passenger has the choice of the exit which will connect him directly with the Glasgow Underground station at Buchanan Street (a nice railway reminder of things past) or he can emerge into George Square. If he takes the latter option he will see that he is standing beside the Copthorne Hotel where, during the war, President Roosevelt's roving emissary, Harry Hopkins, had a vital meeting with British and Allied leaders.

To be more precise it was in that hotel, but then called the North British, that the meeting took place. For close on 100 years the hotel dominated the north side of George Square as a flagship of one of the old Scottish railway companies, and railway enthusiasts cannot but regret the change of name, however euphonious Copthorne may sound.

NOT AN ENGINE IN SIGHT!
Looking into the Station in the early 1950s prior to modernisation.
© The Herald

QUEEN STREET STATION
Gresley D49/1 No. 2760 "Westmorland" backs out from the High Level Station under the signal gantry – 1938
© British Rail/Colour-Rail

EDINBURGH WAVERLEY STATION

There is no competition for the most romantically-named and spectacularly-sited station in Britain, Edinburgh Waverley wins by a mile.

The first station building to be erected in the low cleft which separates Old and New Towns was put up in 1846, when Sir Walter Scott was only recently dead and the fame of *The Wizard of the North* was at its peak.

Subsequently, the station underwent two major re-organisations, by the North British Railway between 1892 and 1902 and by British Rail between 1988–89.

Since Edinburgh had no natural barrier like the Clyde, the line could come into the very heart of the city, literally the "Heart of Midlothian" and the traveller, emerging from the Calton Hill Tunnel from the east, or the Mound Tunnel from the west, suddenly sees the Old Town piled high and theatrically above him.

There is a Law of Compensation at work here because the station itself, currently operating 12 platforms, is not particularly remarkable. Because of a servitude (the Scots equivalent of the English doctrine of Ancient Lights) the station buildings had to be of modest height. There are no great soaring arches or canopies as in Glasgow's Queen Street and Central. The station nevertheless epitomised the romance of railway travel.

Its principal concern is the East Coast main line to King's Cross, London, the route of such famous trains as the *Flying Scotsman*, the *Coronation* and the *Elizabethan*.. North of Edinburgh that line continues with the spectacular crossings of the Forth and Tay Bridges. There is a regular service to Perth, Inverness, Dundee and Aberdeen. The second Glasgow line, one of the old Caley routes through West Lothian and Lanarkshire, shows signs of a recent revival and there is a slightly further than usual commuter link with Dunfermline in the north, North Berwick in the east and Bathgate in the west. Compared with Glasgow, though, the amount of suburban traffic can fairly be described as negligible and Waverley would handle about half the number of movements in a day that Glasgow Central does.

With the electrification of the East Coast Main Line, London is now minutes over four hours away, as opposed to the six hours in which the *Coronation* covered the distance in 1937–1939.

In some aspects, Waverley has been a curiously user-unfriendly station. Overnight passengers from the south are decanted at some considerable distance from the main terminal buildings and securing a taxi has frequently all the characteristics of a scrum, appropriate enough perhaps in the city which boasts Murrayfield as one of its proudest possessions.

For those in search of public transport there is the steep ramp to be negotiated and for the unwary going directly to Princes Street, the steep and Siberian Waverley Steps lie in wait.

Even the approach to the magnificent North British Hotel (now somewhat bafflingly the New Balmoral) had something of the adventurous about it. The arriving guest came up in two creaky and cavernous lifts, walked along booming and empty service corridors adorned with railway posters and pictures from the past and suddenly emerged in the reception area of one of the great hotels of the world.

The view, however, and the sense of theatre, made up and make up for everything. Scott died just before the Railway Age had properly got under way otherwise it might have been of this station that he was thinking when he wrote:-

> *"Breathes there a man with soul so dead*
> *Who never to himself has said*
> *'This is my own, my native land'."*

WAVERLEY STATION

Seen from The Mound in August 1958 with four trains ready to depart plus the J83 pilot.

© C J B Sanderson/Colour-Rail

GLASGOW BUCHANAN STREET STATION

Beyond doubt Buchanan Street was the ugly bairn of the major Glasgow railway stations. Hemmed in by grimy tenements and gaunt warehouses it always seemed that it belonged in spirit to some ghastly Russian provincial town.

There are always those who love their ill-favoured bairns best and Buchanan Street had its devotees. It had started life propitiously in 1849 as the main Caledonian station in the city and for thirty years it was the terminus of the main-line Anglo-Scottish trains on the West Coast route. When it lost out to Central Station on the latter's opening in 1879, it also lost any hope of becoming an elegant structure. Such improvements as were made tended to be with materials cannibalised from other stations.

The canopy and entrance drive were comparatively small-scale although there were one or two discreet concessions to elegance, as in the little office which hired out pillows and rugs for the overnight journeys north.

North was the airt with which Buchanan Street concerned itself, it was essentially the base for trains going to Stirling, Perth, Aberdeen, Dundee, Inverness and Oban. It may well have attracted more Received Pronunciation accents than any of its Glaswegian sisters.

Some of its trains cannot but evoke acute nostalgia. There was the Gleneagles/Crieff and Balquhidder/Callander Express which divided at Dunblane. Somehow the word Express is a contradiction in terms when applied to these somnolent locations.

It was a station where the trains tended to leave in clusters and between-times Buchanan Street could be almost rural. There were various railway curiosities like the parcel trains which twice a day made the circuitous route from Central to Buchanan Street. There was, too, the handful of trains bound for Hamilton, not a common Buchanan Street destination.

Most spectacular of all there were the trace-horses, three hundred of the Caledonian Railway, two hundred of the famous firm of Wordie, which would toil painfully uphill from the city centre and then, unburdened, thunder down West Nile Street under the cavalier guidance of the trace-boys.

Hard perhaps to love a station described in a Glasgow newspaper of 1897 thus:- "Of all the ugly blots upon the Glasgow landscape Buchanan Street railway station stands easily first". Yet it had its moments. It was the last refuge in the early 1960s of the great A4 Pacifics, steaming valiantly in three hours to Aberdeen hauling named expresses like *The Bon Accord, The Saint Mungo* and *The Granite City*.

When the football club of that city reached the Scottish Cup Final, Buchanan Street came alive with thousands of black and gold (later red) supporters in those more good-humoured days.

And for the writer, it was the most marvellous sight he saw in the terrible winter of 1963, after travelling down from Inverness in a train so cold that the food congealed as it was put on the dining-car plates. A noted Scottish football manager and the writer only survived by walking the corridors endlessly from Pitlochry to Glasgow.

That was in 1963 and four short years later the unpretentious workaday station had passed into history. The closure in November 1966 was followed by almost instant demolition although ScotRail House built prior to this stands on an adjoining site.

MORNING DEPARTURE

The train information board announces the departure of the 10 am to Aberdeen while the bill-board in the foreground heralds the station's closure – 1966

© Don Martin, Strathkelvin Libraries

GLASGOW ST ENOCH STATION

St Enoch Station was the successor to Dunlop Street station which of itself was interesting as the first station on the north bank of the Clyde which could receive trains from the south and west by means of the bridge over the river at Hutchesontown.

The project to be undertaken on behalf of the Glasgow & South Western Railway was massive and in its initial stages called for a station with six platforms (this number would subsequently be doubled). The line would come into the very heart of the city in St Enoch Square. There would be a luxury hotel built, of more than 200 bedrooms, and both station and hotel would be electrically lit. The station in fact was to be the first public building in Glasgow to use this means of illumination.

St Enoch opened operationally on 1 May 1876, the day that saw the inauguration of the last of the three main Anglo-Scottish services, the Midland line to London St Pancras over the Settle route. There was a corresponding East of Scotland line from Waverley to St Pancras which ran through Hawick.

Later the English trains from St Enoch would arrive at St Pancras as the *Thames-Clyde Express* but cross-border traffic was not top priority at St Enoch's.

Glasgow & South Western was what the company was called and Glasgow and south-western it meant. A swarming station in the summer, St Enoch despatched thousands of holidaymakers to the Ayrshire coast, to Ayr, Prestwick, Troon, to Ardrossan for Arran, to Largs and Fairlie for Millport, to Princes Pier Greenock for the small holiday hamlets of the Clyde, this last in fierce competition with the Caledonian Railway steamers operating from Gourock but essentially covering the same territory.

Slightly further afield went the *"Glesca Paddy"*, the Irish Express to Stranraer which on the way served Girvan and beyond. There were the commuter lines from Busby and East Kilbride. There was the inter-war phenomenon of the Saturday golf trains, running from eleven o'clock until one on summer mornings, and conveying regiments of golfers to the courses at Barassie, Gailes, Troon and Prestwick. Rumour had it that in the quiet winter months an obliging guard would lock the carriage door on arrival at the course so that the hand of solo could be resumed undisturbed on the return journey.

And yet, for all its handsome frontage, for all the imposing facade of the great hotel, St Enoch was at once overtaken by the Central Station which had opened almost immediately afterwards. When the Prince and Princess of Wales (later Edward VII and Alexandra) had officially opened St Enoch on 17 October 1876, its future seemed assured for generations.

There was no post-war modernisation after 1945 on any scale, itself an ominous sign. There were various efforts made to bolster flagging traffic, for example when the *Starlight Expresses*, the overnight English excursion trains, started up, they were initially allocated in their entirety to St Enoch's as were the first Car Sleepers, which ran through to Marylebone.

It was to no avail. The great hotel, in which the author wrote a television script with the eminent sports writer Hugh McIlvanney in 1973 was from a past age, with its astonishingly high ceilings, and, even then, marble fire places.

The station closed in 1966, a few months before Buchanan Street, and the elegant station, with its great canopy roof and the sharply-curving tracks that were perhaps its most predominant feature, alike fell silent. The hotel staggered on until 1974 when the prohibitive expense involved in meeting the new fire regulations sealed its fate. In one short year Glasgow's stock of mainline stations had been halved.

ST ENOCH STATION & HOTEL

View from St Enoch Square in the early 1900s

© Springburn Museum

GLASGOW CENTRAL STATION

Although the Caledonian line to Glasgow from the south was completed by 1848, the Clyde was to prove an impossible barrier for the next 30 years. During that period the Caledonian line terminated at South Side, out towards Polmadie. Soon after the Glasgow & South Western shared a station at Bridge Street.

The inconvenience of this arrangement became increasingly evident and in 1878 the Caley line was continued into the heart of the city by a viaduct built at a cost of £64,000.

Beyond this viaduct lay the majestic new Central Station, initially of six platforms but later extended to 13 by 1905 at which time it could handle 600 passenger train movements per day. There were also two Low Level platforms which have persisted until today with the exception of a fifteen year gap from 1964.

Central Station is never at rest. Out on the far left flank as one approaches up the steep but well-concealed ascent to the platforms from Gordon Street, are the English expresses on platforms 1 and 2, not only the traditional spectacular London trains, in their heyday the three Scots, *Royal, Mid-Day and Night*, but also expresses for the South Coast of England and the *Cornish Scot* which goes all the way to Penzance. The Inter-City 225 services to London King's Cross via Edinburgh Waverley are a recent introduction.

At the other extremity of the station, the Gourock and Wemyss Bay trains convey passengers to the Lower Firth and link with the ferries at those destinations. From the central platforms the commuters are served, on the Cathcart Circle, the Neilston line, the one by King's Park and Croftfoot to Newton, East Kilbride and Edinburgh via Shotts.

That might seem to be enough for any station to handle, but with the closure of St Enoch in 1966 Central was asked to take some 250 extra trains per day and coped with the extra load without fuss. This took its daily figure of train movements to just under the 1000 mark, making it by the mid-1970s one of the busiest passenger stations in the United Kingdom. It is now used by 100,000 passengers each week day with 850 train movements.

Among lines it inherited were the Irish trains with Stranraer as destination and the Largs and Ayr lines.

In appearance Central was always the lightest and airiest of the four Glasgow stations even in the days of steam, and this has been accentuated further by recent re-decoration and development. The blackened stone of the massive Central Hotel (at one time the obligatory stop of every film star who visited Glasgow) has been lightened, there are high-quality shops on the concourse and above all there is room to move around.

Regrettable casualties there have been, and railway-lovers would deplore most of all the loss of the marvellous curved destination windows which ran along the bow front of the first floor offices. The clever manipulation of painted boards by hand and poles was a distinctive sight and many regarded the "computer print-out" replacement as a poor exchange.

Central Station was part and parcel of Glasgow life. Many a Glaswegian had his or her first romantic tryst at The Shell, the silent reminder of World War I which stood in the middle of the concourse. The passenger who raised his eyes to the wall above could see a more poignant reminder in the massive War Memorial to the employees of the Caledonian Railway who fell in such numbers during that war.

The blend of tradition and development made the Central the absorbing station it is and it pioneered the concept of a Reception Lounge for Rail Sleeper passengers, on the analogy of the comparable airline facility. Over the generations the exiles knew they were home as their train clattered sedately across the bridge and stopped under the great canopy.

Train information display, main concourse – 1983.
Until 1985 these boards dated back to Caley days
© John Peter

MURRAY'S DIARY
The railway traveller's Bible.
Many a Scot on the strength of it
planned exotic trips to such
destinations as Back o' Loch Halt!
© Alan Carlaw

GLASGOW CENTRAL
Britannia class Pacific No. 70052 "Firth of Tay" awaits departure – October 1957
© J L Stevenson

THE EDINBURGH & GLASGOW RAILWAY

For more than a century and a half passenger trains have linked Scotland's two great cities and for over twenty years the main line was in the charge of the Edinburgh & Glasgow Railway, (the order of the cities might be thought to be significant).

This Company got under way in 1842 but there had been attempts to set up a railway before that. Top level advice was sought and indeed George Stephenson himself was involved. He favoured a route by Slamannan and Bathgate instead of the conventional Forth-Clyde route eventually adopted.

When the railway began operations in 1842 the Edinburgh terminal was Haymarket, and still on the present line there survive a few of the original cast-iron mileposts which give distances from Glasgow to that station.

As elsewhere, the canal companies competed fiercely, but not even their introduction of "Swifts", longboats pulled by dashing horses at a pace which in contemporary prints threw up an impressive (and potentially damaging) bow wave, could stem the inevitable supremacy of the new method of transport.

It took 7000 men, many of them Irish navvies, to connect the two cities and many of the Irishmen's difficulties arose with the local inhabitants along the line rather than with the terrain. The line was remarkably flat and with one significant exception there was only one short gradient of 1 in 600, elsewhere it never got above 1 in 800. The exception of course was the first mile out of Queen Street on the very steep 1 in 45 climb to Cowlairs but that was imposed by the intransigence of the Forth and Clyde Navigation Company and the Port Dundas Canal Company rather than any topographical considerations.

The early impoverished traveller by the E & G had to be of a Spartan disposition. Alone of railway companies it offered four classes of transportation and fourth class, in which passengers stood in open trucks was to say the least a gruelling mode of travel. Exposed to the fury of a Scottish winter for 2½ hours on stopping trains, the numbed and sooty passengers must have given heartfelt thanks as eventually they alighted.

Mercifully, as quickly as 1848, the time taken by non-stop trains had come down to 1½ hours and astonishingly, over the next hundred years this time would improve by only 11 minutes on normal service!

The Edinburgh & Glasgow line was assiduously promoted. One of the most imaginative schemes was designed to encourage settlement along the railway route. To this end incentives were offered to those who would build houses. The builder of a house at Lenzie to the value of £1000 would receive free travel for 10 years and a sliding scale operated. Lenzie flourished and at least one "ticket house" remains to be seen today. Lenzie flourished, but Dullatur stayed a village.

From the outset there were Sunday trains, perhaps surprisingly. Less surprisingly there was fierce opposition to them. The Rev William Chalmers Burns of Kilsyth was a noted opponent and he was wont to describe Sunday trains as "A reward for Sabbath-breaking: people taken swiftly and safely to Hell!" Initially at least the Sabbatarians had their way, Sunday services were withdrawn in 1846 and were not restored until 1865.

For the first four years of its existence the E & G Railway ran in splendid isolation from Queen Street and then the line was pushed on from Haymarket to Waverley in 1846. Junction with the Caledonian came two years later at Greenhill near Bonnybridge in Stirlingshire.

In earlier days the line was important for coal-carrying and later for the short-lived Scottish shale-oil industry but it was always pre-eminently a fast passenger line.

Some expresses went further afield. There was the Fifeshire Coast Express and the Lothian Coast Express which took Glaswegians on holiday to the East Coast resorts, but the inter-city traffic has always been sufficiently numerous to be self-standing. Today there is a half-hourly service between the cities.

The E & G route was assumed by the LNER at the grouping in 1923 with British Railways taking over after the Second World War. Steam gave way to the Swindon Class 126 diesels in 1957 and the use of Class 27 diesels in pairs in 1971 reduced the running time to 43 minutes, although this demanding timetable was observed with some considerable difficulty. For a short time the Class 27s were replaced by 47/7s until in September 1991 the Class 158 diesels made not only their Scottish but also their British debut. These were the first purpose-built units on the line since the early diesels of 1957. The route is now a candidate for electrification.

Over the years the line has conveyed crowds to Murrayfield in one direction, Hampden in the other, Edinburgh Festival-goers in the evenings of September and, all year round, it seems that the legal profession in its entirety is going in both directions on the early morning trains.

THE ALMOND VIADUCT

By far the most striking feature of the Edinburgh & Glasgow Railway was the Almond Viaduct which was started in 1838 and took almost three years to complete.
It is a most graceful structure of 36 arches, each 70 feet high and having a span of 50 feet and even in the earliest years of Victoria it cost an impressive £130,000.
Today it is fortunately recognised for the masterpiece of railway architecture that it is and the viaduct is classed as a listed building, Grade A.

(Painting by D O Hill at time of opening of viaduct - courtesy Glasgow Museum of Transport)

THE CATHCART CIRCLE

This year Scotland's most famous commuter line, the Cathcart Circle, celebrates its centenary. The various Scottish railways had by 1894 tied up pretty thoroughly all inter-city and cross-border traffic and it was now time to look after the burgeoning suburbs of the Second City of the Empire.

There were two aspirants to build the new line from Central Station to Cathcart and had either of the Glasgow South Suburban Railway Company's proposals been adopted then the Circle would have been much smaller than the line eventually built by the other applicant, the Cathcart District Railway Company. In particular the three western stations of Shawlands, Maxwell Park and Pollokshields West would have been missing from the final selected route. Trains had been running to Cathcart since 1886, which was strangely enough the year of the opening of G & J Weir's pump factory at Cathcart which until today could make a strong claim to be the most important industrial concern in the Circle's immediate catchment area.

The building of the line caused some upheaval. Queen's Park Football Club had to move their ground across Cathcart Road to what would later be Cathkin Park, home of Third Lanark Football Club. The elegant flats of Pollokshields – who would dare call them tenements? – followed the new line and by 1910 there were desirable residences all round the circumference of the Circle.

To use a then current Glasgow word, the clientele was "select". The male travellers were bowler-hatted and wore tailored coats, the ladies described themselves as "being out at business". Although the route lay through heavily built-up suburbs there was a peculiarly rustic air to the Circle, the city did not impinge. Home for lunch was a possibility.

During the First World War two of the stations, Crosshill and Langside, suffered lengthy closures in what was one of the more bizarre wartime economies. Both lay shuttered and empty for two years.

My own association with the Circle goes back to 1934. Mount Florida was then the football capital of the world. On International and Cup Final days fifteen trains an hour would disgorge their passengers for Hampden on the wooden extension to the platform which ran for more than 400 yards. From my house late at night high above the line I could see the sparks of the engines as they plodded round the loop to King's Park and Croftfoot which had opened in 1928 and 1931 respectively to serve these new dormitory districts.

In the Second World War the Circle rendered sterling service as petrol became scarcer and delivery vans vanished from the roads. Almost all the southside evening papers came out by train and I travelled every day by the Circle for the six years of the war.

Most of the labour was done by sturdy tank engines but just now and then to our delight we got an engine with tender. As boys we instinctively felt these to be better, rather as Italian immigrants to the United States were said to be lured by drawings of four-funnelled liners.

Who can forget the heavy door handles, the thick leather straps which had to be jerked slightly inwards to allow the window to fall, the bench seats of uncut mocquette and the sepia pictures of such pre-war holiday resorts as Gleneagles, Southport and Grange-over-Sands?

The smell of the gaslamps at Pollokshaws East is in my nostrils yet as I recall stumbling up the last few steps for the 8.49 am to Crosshill. As we scrambled aboard we admired the Olympian detachment with which the guard casually swung himself onto the running board before disappearing into the holy of holies, the guard's van.

By the Fifties the lights were back and the steam trains were going but not before they were called upon to buy time for the railway after an embarrassing first failure of the diesels in 1958. The line was electrified in 1962.

Inevitably unmanned stations have led to the Circle becoming more unkempt. There have been a couple of bad fires at Langside and Pollokshields East, the last a station which made melancholy headlines when one of its staff was shot dead in a robbery in 1945. The staff remain important however and there are many like Archie McAreavey at Crosshill who can truly be said to be guide and mentor to their customers, and without whose sapient advice no long rail journey should be contemplated.

The Circle had its own muse, R W Campbell's Snooker Tam ,and Tam's creator put more succinctly than anyone the benefits conferred by this venerated railway line: "God made the country, man made the cities and the railways made the suburbs."

MAXWELL PARK STATION

The original building, now unstaffed, is basically intact although showing signs of its age. A class 303 EMU arrives on an Outer Circle train in March 1994

© Alan Carlaw

THE WEST HIGHLAND RAILWAY

If one were pedantic, the West Highland Railway proper is the 99 miles between Craigendoran Junction and Fort William and it is this section which will celebrate its centenary on 11 August 1994. In the popular mind however the West Highland line stretches 206 miles and almost certainly includes the Oban line and the extension to Mallaig which did not open until 1901.

The Marchioness of Tweeddale performed the opening ceremony in August 1894, when the "Oban Times", never a journal to use one cliche where three would do, reported the event thus:- "Now however by means of the iron horse, the worthy citizens of Glasgow and Edinburgh may partake of a late breakfast at home and still be able to enjoy a comfortable early dinner in far Lochaber under the frowning shadow of Ben Nevis, the monarch of British mountains."

In the construction of the West Highland Railway two major obstacles had to be faced, the difficulty of terrain and the astonishing remoteness of much of the line. It almost passes belief that within 100 miles of Glasgow there were stations such as Rannoch, Corrour and Gorton so isolated that the railway staff stationed there had to be supplied with everything they needed by train, much as the tiny stations dotting the Nullarbor Desert in Australia are provisioned by the famous Tea and Sugar train.

Weather posed and continues to pose major problems, The very first surveying party over Rannoch Moor, one of Europe's great wildernesses, was almost wiped out in 1889 by a near fatal under-estimation of the ferocity of a Scottish winter. The brain of the surveyors plus the muscle and dogged devotion of the navvies threw a line across the seemingly impenetrable Rannoch Moor, whose desolation is so tellingly described in Stevenson's "Kidnapped" and Neil Munro's marvellous "John Splendid". The solution to the boggy moor was Sherman's solution to the Carolina swamps, "Corduroy'em!", that is, rely heavily on floating the tracks on brushwood.

There are of course railways elsewhere in the world which overcame obstacles of a more Homeric kind, one thinks of the Chihuahua Pacifico in Mexico, the Bolivian Railway of the high Alto Plano and the sub-continental line which chugs up to the old hill-station of the British Army at Simla.

The West Highland Railway certainly represents one of the major European challenges with a station at Corrour more than 1000 feet up, a snow shed at Cruach and blizzards which in 1895 completely covered the snowplough engine at Roy Bridge and extinguished its fire.

The building of the railway was a wonderful feat of engineering. It was not only the set pieces, the 12 tunnels, the 617 bridges, the imposing Glenfinnan viaduct almost 420 yards long which with its 21 massive arches sets off the lonely glen as if it had always been planned that man would build it there.

The line is loved for its eccentricities, so that a station, Taynuilt, is furnished with its own brewery and a handful of houses at Tyndrum, which might be considered inordinately lucky to have a station in modern times, has in fact two.

The West Highland has never been a line for greyhounds, topography alone would see to that, but the four hours to Fort William for the 121 miles from Glasgow represented a saving of more than two days when the line was opened. Just over 150 years had elapsed since the hanging of a son of Rob Roy and well into the eighteenth century lowland merchants embarking on a business trip to the Highlands made their wills as a prudent precaution.

The West Highland Line has conferred two great benefits on Scotland. To many small and isolated communities it has been a literal lifeline and it has enabled generations of Lowlanders to appreciate what an astonishingly beautiful country they inhabit. As the train trundles along high terraces on mountain-sides, as the line shows desolate tracts of moor, imposing mountains and occasional cultivated land in a glen, as on the final stretch the deep lochs give tantalising glimpses of the far-out islands, it is indeed an unperceptive traveller who would not offer a silent prayer of thanks to those Victorian giants whose brain and muscle built the West Highland tracks. Slainte!

LEAVING GLENFINNAN
Gresley K2 No. 61791 pilots No. 61995 "Cameron of Lochiel" out of Glenfinnan
with a down Mallaig mixed train – March 1956
© J M Jarvis/Colour-Rail

CRIANLARICH
Thompson B1 No. 61336 in LNER apple green crossing the Strathfillan Viaduct
with a freight for Fort William – August 1948
© K H Leech/Colour-Rail

THE FORTH BRIDGE

On 4 March 1890, His Royal Highness the Prince of Wales, later King Edward VII, who had just driven in the last rivet on the Forth Bridge made a speech at the subsequent lunch. He mentioned that the extreme length of the bridge was 2,765 yards, that the weight of steel was 51,000 tons, that approximately eight million rivets had been used, that the rail level above high water was 156 feet and that 42 miles of bent plate had been used in the tubes, the distance between Edinburgh and Glasgow.

He might have mentioned another grimmer statistic, that 57 of the 4,500 men employed had been killed, but this was not the occasion for that. It would have given some idea of the immensity of the project but none of the grandeur of the finished product.

But for the collapse of the first Tay Bridge the Forth would have been spanned a decade earlier. Work had begun in 1873 on a bridge designed by Thomas Bouch but his credibility vanished when the high-girdered bridge over the Tay collapsed and the Forth project was abandoned.

Victorians were extraordinarily buoyant with an innate sense of "can-do" and in 1883 work was recommenced to the design of Benjamin Baker with John Fowler as Consulting Engineer and William Arrol as Contractor.

Arrol epitomised what we like to think of in Scotland as "the lad o'pairts". At one time an apprentice blacksmith he saved prodigiously to establish himself in business in the east end of Glasgow. Gradually the major railway companies entrusted him with important commissions, notably the new bridge which brought the Caledonian over the Clyde into Central Station. In the 1880s the former Renfrewshire apprentice would carry responsibility for the building of the Forth Bridge and the re-building of the Tay Bridge simultaneously!

The building of this mighty bridge, on the cantilever principle which had been known for centuries in the Far East, was to take seven years. Mild steel would be used, rather than the cast iron of the ill-fated bridge to the north. There was great pressure for the estuary to be bridged, especially from the North British Railway Company which until this was accomplished would be severely disadvantaged in the Race to the North beyond Edinburgh. The little hamlets of North and South Queensferry became shanty towns as the thousands of workers flocked in although their behaviour was almost universally praised by those in charge of the project.

Gradually the three cantilever towers climbed to their height of 361 feet and the two main spans of 1,710 feet each took shape. Foreign interest was intense. The Emperor of Brazil, the Shah of Persia and the Kings of Belgium, Sweden and Saxony all came to visit and impeded progress to different degrees.

In the wake of the Tay Bridge disaster the Government had insisted that there should be continuous and independent monitoring of progress by the Board of Trade and one of the two men appointed to oversee the work was Major Francis Marindin of the Royal Engineers. He would have been known to some of the work force at least since he had played in two FA Cup Finals and later refereed several more, in two of which the famous Scottish side, Queen's Park, were involved.

We think of Victorian times as being repressive and restrictive for women but this was not the case for the well-to-do. The first authorised walk over the bridge on 15 October 1889 was led by Miss Constance Taylor, niece of the Marchioness of Tweeddale and that lady was to go one better by driving the first train over the bridge (the first official train that is) because from January 1890 the bridge had been tested by driving heavy goods trains over it and deliberately stopping them out in the middle.

No Victorian occasion was complete without its quota of royalty and aristocracy but it is fair to say that one man, M Gustave Eiffel, might have been casting a more knowledgeable eye on opening day.

So the bridge was finished, in less than seven years and quickly passed into Scottish life and legend. Every Scottish pupil knew that 29 men were employed to do nothing else but paint the bridge continuously. Modern invention has cut this crew to only four but the four still use paint supplied by the original company, Craig and Rose of Leith.

World-wide exposure came with the 1930s when the first and best version of John Buchan's "Thirty Nine Steps" featured a thrilling scene with Robert Donat on the bridge itself. There was further if unwanted fame when, in October 1939, the first German aircraft to be destroyed in the Second World War was brought down during an attack on the Forth Bridge.

It might have been thought that the opening of the much more intensively-used Forth Road Bridge would have diminished the status of the older crossing, but Arrol's bridge went triumphantly to its centenary in March 1990 although there was not universal approbation for the tricking-out of the centenarian with lights.

The bridge remains an astonishing example of Victorian skill, drive and courage. It was the boast of many a working man in Scotland as the last century closed that in the words of the folk-song "I helped to build the mighty bridge that spans the busy Forth".

HOME TERRITORY
Sole survivor of the LNER A2 class No. 60532 " Blue Peter" crosses the Forth Bridge with a steam excursion on 17 October 1993
© Chris Kapolka
Inset – The bridge under construction in the 1880s
© Scottish Records Office

THE TAY BRIDGE DISASTER

There have been few more dramatic happenings in the entire railway history of the world than the collapse of the Tay Bridge as a train passed over it on the last Sunday evening of 1879. A ferocious storm of wind, developing from nothing so that what had been a flat calm at two o'clock was a genuine hurricane five hours later, swept the last train from Edinburgh off the bridge at the high girders.

The Tay Bridge was a recent construction, less than two years had passed since Queen Victoria declared it opened in May 1878 and knighted the man in charge, Thomas Bouch. At two miles it was the longest in the world and its slender structure spanned the Tay gracefully.

On that ill-omened night the 4.15 from Edinburgh moved remorselessly to its doom. More accurately the train was the 5.27 from Burntisland for as yet the Forth remained unbridged and needed a ferry crossing. There had been portents. Regular users of the Tay Bridge had complained of excessive vibration, recent inspections had shown cracks in the main pillars. This was in the month of December but Sir Thomas Bouch knew that similar developments had occurred with other new bridges and the offending pillars were simply secured with iron hoops.

No novel could have evoked such a situation. There was an astonishing escape for one of the passengers, a Mr Linskill, who had arranged for a carriage to meet him at Leuchars to take him to St Andrews. It was not there when the train arrived and he decided to carry on to Dundee and put up there overnight. The train lingered at Leuchars for a few moments while the wheels were inspected, the guard and station-master took a last look-out, the carriage lights were seen far down the road and Linskill lived.

There was too an element of the supernatural. Far away in East Lothian at the time of the actual disaster a farmer, ashen-faced, said to his friend, "I have just seen the Tay Bridge go down." They were returning from church and many Sabbatarians were not slow in imputing the tragedy to the impious decision of the railways to run Sunday trains.

The last men to see the ill-fated Cowlairs engine, No. 224, and its carriages were the signal box staff on the south side of the river as the baton which would give the train the line was handed to the fireman. Then the train took the bridge in the howling blast and as it entered the high girders it presented the wind with a solid object on which to exert its appalling force. The train plummeted to the river bed. There were no survivors.

Total confusion reigned. Men on both sides of the estuary thought they had seen lights plunging off the bridge but not even the signalmen on either side knew what had happened for some considerable time. The actual tragedy was bad enough but first garbled reports, emitted in panic from the N.B. head office in Edinburgh, put the death rate at 300, well beyond the carrying capacity of the train.

There were some macabre postscripts. The engine, No. 224, was retrieved from the river bed and returned to service. The railwaymen with gallows humour re-christened it "The Diver" and it is reputed to have been used as the logo for the Cowlairs Co-operative Society.

There was one other casualty in addition to the 73 passengers and train crew. Within a year Sir Thomas Bouch was dead, nervous strain said the doctors, broken heart said his family and friends.

Ten years later the Tay had been bridged again and shortly afterwards the Forth. Leave the last word with a prominent Dundonian, William McGonagall, who knew that the set-back to engineering confidence was only temporary:–

"Oh ill-fated Bridge of the Silv'ry Tay,
I must now conclude my lay,
By telling the world fearlessly without the least dismay,

That your central girders would not have given way.
At least sensible men do say,
Had they been supported on each side with buttresses,

At least many sensible men confesses,
For the stronger we our houses do build,
The less chance we have of being killed."

THE HIGH GIRDERS

Line engraving from a photograph taken at low water of the fallen girders to illustrate an article in "Engineer" of 30 January 1880

SCOTTISH RAILWAY COMPANY INSIGNIA

THE HIGHLAND RAILWAY

The heraldic symbolism of this is the carrying of the line across the Grampians from Perth to Inverness. Presided over by a none too benign looking eagle, the two burgh coats of arms regard each other somewhat uneasily. On the left is the Lamb and Banner which traditionally represented St John as the Lion does St Mark. This is a reminder, re-inforced by the city's football team, that Perth was for long known as St John's Town with the rallying cry "Hey for bonny St Johnston." The Inverness coat of arms very unusually depicts Christ on the Cross and there is thus a strongly evangelical theme to this blazon which with traditional thrift was reserved only for mainline passenger engines.

THE GREAT NORTH OF SCOTLAND RAILWAY

The name of this railway was always misleading as it had Scotland's smallest track mileage and was effectively confined to the plains of Buchan and the Moray Firth. Only on the Royal Deeside line from Aberdeen to Ballater were mountains to be seen which were worthy of the name. In the coat of arms both facets of the company's operation were commemorated, the three silver towers of the City of Aberdeen being quartered with the Lion Rampant of Scotland. Even Homer nods they say and certainly the incumbent Lyon King of Arms must have been dozing to overlook this flagrant disregard of the exclusivity of kingly symbols. But, as a certain Mr Durante, not noted for an interest in heraldry was to say a generation later "You ain't heard nothing yet."

THE CALEDONIAN RAILWAY

Hitler's henchman, Dr Joseph Goebbels was noted for his reliance on the big lie, the theory being that people would swallow the deception if it were sufficiently monumental. Certainly the Caledonian must have reasoned that if you were going to breach the restrictions on using other people's coats of arms, then do not borrow here and there but use them in their entirety. As a result and possibly in an attempt to obscure the fact that much English money was backing the line from Carlisle north, the arms of the Caley were simply the Royal Arms of Scotland. There is no more to be said except that when scores of people have been hauled before the Lyon Court for the minutest of infractions, however did the Caley get away with such heraldic larceny?

THE GLASGOW & SOUTH WESTERN RAILWAY

Of all the five Scottish-based railways this is by far the most interesting coat of arms since it is essentially that of the Glasgow, Paisley, Kilmarnock and Ayr Railway which goes back to the pioneering railway days of 1837. Visually it is by far the most imaginative in its demands upon the reader of the Classics, incorporating as it does the symbols of two gods and a goddess. Mercury is represented by the caduceus or winged staff, denoting him as the messenger of the gods and therefore concerned with speed. In the centre is the distaff of Minerva, goddess of industry and on the right is the trident of Neptune, an appropriate reference to the Ayrshire ports given the very early connections between the Dukes of Portland and the colliery tramways to the sea. The three devices are bonded by a crown.

It is interesting to note that the mythology theme was carried over by the Glasgow & South Western to their fleet of paddle steamers, each of the three deities named here being commemorated in this fashion. The second paddler which bore the name Mercury, an LMS boat by that time, was sunk in 1940 while on war service as a minesweeper.

THE NORTH BRITISH RAILWAY

North Britain was the official designation of Scotland in the early days of railways and the postal service. Even newspapers bore such titles as The North British Daily Mail. The title was used without umbrage by such patriotic Scots as Sir Charles Tennant.

The particular claim to fame of the North British Railway among the historic Scottish foundations was that it had been the first to cross the English border. Thus the coat of arms depicts the emblems of Edinburgh and Berwick-on-Tweed and for those who need a further nudge to appreciate heraldic thinking, the national emblems of the thistle and the rose are also represented.

In the company's later days, when it had extended operations to the West Highlands of Scotland, this insignia conveyed a somewhat limited view of the NB's workings but the coat of arms remained unchanged until the grouping of 1923.

SCOTTISH RAILWAY INSIGNIA

THE STOBCROSS CRANE

For generations of Glaswegians the Stobcross Crane has been one of the city's leading landmarks. Few referred to it as such in conversation, it remained the original "Finnieston" crane, and the phrase came to be used for anything or anyone of Homeric proportions, "their centre-half is built like the Finnieston crane!"

Even before 1914 there had been talk of the need for the Clyde to be bridged further west. Finnieston was the site initially preferred but the project foundered on the fact that a low-level fixed bridge would mean the end of upstream traffic. At that time river steamers still left from the Broomielaw; the famous Clyde "puffers" could be seen moored at Stockwell Bridge, MacBrayne's used the Kingston Dock for much of their cargo traffic to the Western Isles and the well-loved Irish boats left from Lancefield Quay. A low-level fixed bridge would put all these in imminent jeopardy, a swing bridge would be far too disruptive to traffic.

In 1926 a proposal was made to have a high-level fixed bridge with a 76 foot clearance at maximum high tide. The recession of the 1930s and then the Second World War held back this undertaking for more than forty years and when the bridge was eventually built it was on a site slightly up-river.

In the meantime however it had been decided to locate the Finnieston crane some 200 yards down-river and in 1932 a new crane, electrically operated and built by Cowans, Sheldon and Co Ltd had come into operation. The money for it was largely provided by the Corporation of Glasgow.

This successor to the steam crane of 1895 was a veritable Goliath, 175 feet high, the horizontal jib 152 feet, the weight capable of being lifted 175 tons. An auxiliary hoist could cope with thirty ton lifts and a jigger hoist could move five ton light loads.

This new provision was invaluable to the Glasgow locomotive manufacturing companies, especially those on the north side of the river. The giant crane had other tasks, the lifting of ships' boilers and engines for example, but in the minds of Glaswegians it was indelibly associated with the swinging aboard of locomotives.

Pre-1939 a Sunday treat for Glasgow children was "to go down the docks" perhaps taking the Plantation Street ferry across the river, then walking along the quays on the other side before returning by the Govan ferry. A great thrill was to see six or more locomotives lined up on the dockside awaiting shipment to Palestine, Egypt, South Africa, China, India....... the destinations were innumerable. Alongside the quay steamers with locomotives already shipped seemed far too small for the task and certain to overturn, but with practically no exceptions the shipments would arrive safely to bring a piece of industrial Scotland to the other side of the globe.

Perhaps the locomotive which attracted most attention while in the vicinity of the crane was one which never turned a wheel in its life. In 1987, fully 25 years after the North British Locomotive Company closed its doors, a Scottish artist, George Wyllie, had the marvellous idea of suspending a straw locomotive from the crane to commemorate the time when Glasgow was the locomotive capital of Europe and well-nigh the world. After its period of suspension above the river, there was even the more poetic notion of taking the locomotive up to the waste railway ground at Springburn to be given a Viking funeral. This journey, the reverse of hundreds made by shining-new locomotives as they were hauled by steam-traction engines or later the Pickford's low-loaders could be said to be the final memorial service for the great locomotive-manufacturing industry of Glasgow. Almost exactly a century after that manufacture peaked, the Stobcross or Finnieston crane remains as a lone and silent witness, looming over an eerily-quiet river. "The hammer's ding-dong is the song of the Clyde". No more.

CRANE BY NIGHT

Floodlit, the crane is now a feature of the north bank adjoining the Scottish Exhibition Centre. The northern rotunda of the first Clyde Tunnel can be seen below the jibs.
© The Herald

CRANE BY DAY

Typical of many loads are these 4-8-2 oil-burning locomotives for the Sudan Government Railways, part of an order for 42, being hoisted on-board ship in August 1955
© Mitchell Library

LNER No. 2511 "Silver King" in garter blue livery looking towards King's Cross loco yard where N2 No. 4725 rests – 1938
© National Railway Museum/Colour-Rail

Waverley Station east end with A3 No.2747 "Coronach" on the Thames-Forth Express, A4 No.4490 "Dominion of Canada" (with bell) on the up Flying Scotsman and a grubby J83 station pilot No. 9830 – August 1939
© The Pendragon Collection/Colour-Rail

LNER B1 4-6-0 No. 1134 in apple green livery at Elgin in 1948
© J M Jarvis/Colour-Rail

ex-CR McIntosh 0-4-4T No. 55169 leaves Glasgow Central with a Cathcart Inner Circle train in the 1950s
© W F Cameron Collection

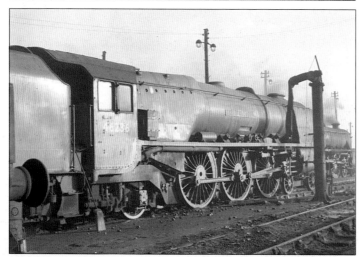

Winter sunshine glints on Stanier Pacific No. 46236 "City of Bradford" as it rests at Polmadie on Christmas day 1963
© Dugald Cameron

No. 46256 "Sir William A Stanier FRS" waits to depart with a return football special from Glasgow Central in April 1964
© Dugald Cameron

A4 No. 60024 "Kingfisher" approaches Buchanan Street with the 1.30 ex-Aberdeen in 1965
© Dugald Cameron

The glory of steam!
A2 No. 60528 "Tudor Minstrel" being serviced at St Margaret's shed in 1965
© Dugald Cameron

Caledonian Railway No. 123 with the two preserved Caledonian coaches approaches Edinburgh Princes Street with an excursion on 19 April 1965
© Dugald Cameron

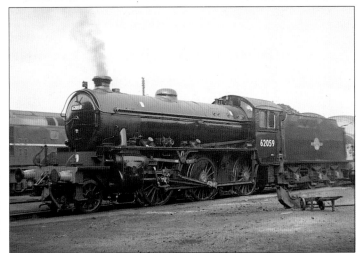

The last steam locomotive to be overhauled by BR in Scotland was K1 class No. 62059. Originally built by NB Loco at its Queen's Park works in December 1949 it left Cowlairs on 22 September 1966 and is seen at Eastfield
© Dugald Cameron

An SRPS excursion to Mallaig seen on the Glenfinnan viaduct in 1986 is hauled by a class 37 diesel
© John Peter

Restored CR McIntosh '812' class 0-6-0 No. 828 about to leave Boat of Garten for Aviemore on the Strathspey Railway in August 1993
© Alan Carlaw

Index

Subjects selected by Dugald Cameron, Ann Glen, Willie Dewar, Alan Carlaw

Cover artwork by Dugald Cameron

Front cover – North British Railway No. 256 *Glen Douglas* heads for Fort William over the Strathfillan Viaduct at Crianlarich in NB days

Rear cover – Wemyss Bay Station in the early 1920s with a Caledonian Railway '944' class 4-6-2T having arrived with a train from Glasgow

Acknowledgements

Ian Gordon - Glasgow Room, Mitchell Library, Glasgow; Don Martin - Strathkelvin Libraries; William Caldwell - ScotRail;
Bill Howie - Hunslet–Barclay, Kilmarnock; Frances Shaw - Scottish Records Office; Trustees of the J F McEwan Collection;
Margaret Cameron; Dugald Cameron; Ann Glen; Alan Carlaw; Elpeeko Ltd; Lord Whitelaw
Alan Glen - Sales & Marketing Manager, Glasgow Royal Concert Hall; Moira Thorburn - Photographic Dept, Mitchell Library, Glasgow

Although every effort has been made to clear copyright, in some cases it has been difficult to trace copyright holders. The publishers apologise for any omissions.